Where I Am Going

Where I Am Going

EXCERPTS FROM THE SPEECHES OF

Jacqueline Grennan

McGraw-Hill Book Company
New York   Toronto   London   Sydney

Library of Congress Catalog Card Number: 68–24342
First Edition   24670

Acknowledgment is made to the following sources for permission
to quote from material already published:

From "What I Believe," copyright © 1939, 1967 by E. M. Forster.
Reprinted from his volume *Two Cheers for Democracy* by permission of Harcourt, Brace & World, Inc.

The Future of Man by Pierre Teilhard de Chardin, 1964. Reprinted by permission of Harper & Row, Inc.

The speech given before the National Conference of Association of
College Admissions Counselors, October 6, 1966, was originally
published by the Journal of the Association of College Admissions
Counselors, Vol. 12, no. 2, and reprinted by permission.

for the life-giving and sharing
of my mother and father,
Francetta, and JRZ

It's where I am going that's important; not where I am.
                                    —October 6, 1964

Contents

Prologue

*The founding of an institution is always
a radical move, a somewhat revolutionary move.*

[This address (November 21, 1966) records the progress and decisions that led Jacqueline Grennan and Webster College to meet the challenge of life outside a religious order. These are historic statements of "one moment in time," pointing new directions for religious-owned institutions. More important, however, they serve as a prologue to the thinking of one individual who, in what Jacqueline Grennan considers an *evolutionary* world, can—and must—lever change.]

—*Publisher's Note*

Every rational system, every constitutional government, every institutional form has been forged out of the new and growing experience of men.   —*June 4, 1967*

Convocation Address
Webster College
November 21, 1966

Unlike most colleges and universities, Webster has not initiated celebration of a Founders' Day. Perhaps it has been a fortunate oversight. I would speculate that those visionary ones who found an institution would be the first to ask that every day be Founders' Day, that every generation be founding a new institution, an aggregate of elements reassembled and reordered best to meet and serve the problems and the promises of *this* day.

In an article published in 1962 for International Business Machines, Mr. John Gardner, then President of the Carnegie Corporation and later Secretary of Health, Education and Welfare, formulated what was to become one of the central

3

thesis questions of this century. Mr. Gardner said: "In the long stretch of history societies have emerged, flourished and died. Over shorter periods organizations emerge, flourish and die." Mr. Gardner goes on to ask if this is inevitable, if this means that there is "no alternative to becoming stiff in the joints." John Gardner called the alternative he proposed in his 1962 paper the principle of the self-renewing society. It is, I believe, the alternative forged by the event of John XXIII, an alternative which was to become known as *aggiornamento*. It is the alternative, I believe, proposed over and over in the Gospel: the seed that must go into the ground and die in order to bring forth new fruit; the new wine that will burst the old wineskins; the Old and New Testament gift of prophecy which always proclaims a new age.

Why is any institution founded? I submit that worthwhile institutions are founded by groups of people coming together in a new way to do something needed by society which older institutions of the society are not prepared to cope with. Thus, the founding of an institution is always a radical move, a somewhat revolutionary move. If the persons involved were thoroughly satisfied with existing institutions, they would see no necessity to found a new one. The new one is almost always conceived to deal with a specific task. It enlists members who become interested in still newer tasks.

At such times in the history of institutions one company often becomes a parent company by generating one or more subsidiaries.

An institution is, indeed, vital when it gives birth to a daughter corporation and nurtures that corporation. It may be most vital of all when the parent institution releases the daughter corporation in its own maturity to its own life. Strong parents, great progenitors are seldom possessive. They seem not to need to live through their children, fulfilled rather in the knowledge that the children can live an independent life—a life willed and generated and fostered by the parent.

Webster College is such an institution, such a corporation—willed to life, generated, nurtured, and fostered by the Sisters of Loretto. Let me trace for you and with you in the next few minutes our family tree.

In 1812 in the hills of Kentucky, three young women began a school in a log cabin. They had come to Kentucky with the early pioneers. Realizing that there were no schools on the frontier, they founded their first log-cabin institution to begin to educate in some rudimentary way their own nieces and nephews and all children in the settlement. That log cabin was *the* school of the neighborhood, open to and concerned about all who would come.

Next, the three young foundresses of a school went about founding an American religious congregation that would speak to and for the new nineteenth-century American frontier. Encouraged and ever pressed to go to Europe for novitiate training as religious, or to bring European religious to Kentucky to train them, they somehow prevailed in their determination to invent a religious community in the very character of the new frontier.

The Sisters of Loretto, like most new corporations, was conceived in the attempt to bring a community of concerned persons together to accomplish a task that the existing society was not yet ready to handle. The community attracted new members and the task grew more extensive.

The next great period of growth in the congregation occurred in the latter part of the nineteenth century when the next generations of Lorettines went farther west with the new pioneers. Again, there was a task of founding schools in the wild and woolly Southwest. And so they went in covered wagons, abandoned cloister, slept on the open prairie, lost one young member in an Indian attack and one to cholera—in order to go where no other teachers would then go, to found schools for the settlers in a community, to accomplish a task that the existing society was not yet ready to handle. Before that century was over, a small boy sat in one of those schools in New Mexico and learned from his own pioneer mother gratitude for that devotion to the spirit of the frontier by these Sisters of Loretto.

We assemble as a community today in the building born of that gratitude and bearing the names of the small boy, Conrad Hilton, and the pioneer Sisters of Loretto who went to found his schools when no one else would go.

Some frontiers are geographic. Others are social, intellectual, and even spiritual. In 1915 a new generation of Sisters of Loretto addressed themselves to a new task. In 1915, college education for women west of the Mississippi was a rare phenomenon, and there was no real Catholic involvement in those few colleges which had opened their doors to the world of women. Again, a new daughter corporation was formed—a subsidiary company of the parent company. Again a community of concerned persons came together to accomplish a task that the existing society was not yet ready to handle. Again, the community attracted new members as the task grew more extensive. But this time, the members of the daughter company began to come from many rich and varied backgrounds. The project launched by the family corporation, the Sisters of Loretto, first even known as Loretto College, became Webster College, and the family corporation became more and more a public corporation. As the task expanded, the Sisters hired cooks and janitors and secretaries and part-time and full professors and top administrators to share in the building of the corporation. It is a story told in many versions. Sometimes we call it the American dream—the small beginning planted by an individual, often rooted by a family, but almost always nurtured and transplanted and crossbred by the wider society that inherits the land.

Some families have held onto their corporations, have refused ever to commit them to the public sector. But these have not been the corporations that have become the leaders of today and the makers of tomorrow. A few decades ago, two chemical companies in St. Louis each had gross sales of under $50 million annually. One, still a family corporation, still operates at about that level. The other, operating in the open world of the public sector, is grossing nearly a billion and a half.

Is Webster College at this moment a family corporation of the Sisters of Loretto or a corporation operating in the open world of the public sector? Legally, like 90 per cent of the Catholic colleges and universities in this country, it is owned and operated by the religious congregation. Sisters of Loretto make up less than 1 per cent of the staff, about 4 per cent of the student body, about 25 per cent of the teaching faculty, 60 per cent of the central administration, and 100 per cent of the legal Board of Directors. As the faculty and many of the older students know, we have for almost three years been questioning seriously the viability of this governmental structure. Some very important questions are raised: (1) Should a General Council of a religious congregation, elected primarily to address itself to the task of operating that congregation, be *ex officio* the Board of Directors of a subsidiary corporation in which the task has become highly diversified and complex? (2) Should an institution of higher education necessarily committed to free inquiry and the frontiers of secular as well as theological knowledge be owned by a congregation which has freely subjected itself to hierarchical control? (3) In the world of Vatican II with its emphasis on involvement of the laity and on ecumenism, might not a dynamically Catholic institution be "catholic" in its original sense of universal—truly ecumenical rather than self-consciously denominational?

This last question was raised quite forcefully, I believe, in a very perceptive editorial in a recent issue of the student newspaper. In this latter operational sense I think many of us believe that Webster is already operating in the open world of the public sector. It is this fact, I believe, which is our glory and our shame. It is the *fact* which impels John Cogley in the *Saturday Review* and Michael Novak in *The Saturday Evening Post* to single us out as one of the most dynamic Catholic colleges in the country. (It is also the *fact* which causes conservative Catholics in California and Kentucky to write me letters to tell me I am a daughter of Beelzebub and each day they pray for my excommunication before nightfall so I won't cause any more trouble.) One learns to thank God for the shared insight of the Cogleys and Novaks. But one learns also to be compassionate with the conservative critics who are compelled to judge the inventions of today by the artifacts of yesterday. Catholic colleges and universities across the country are soul-searching about their mission in the new intellectual and spiritual frontier that my generation has begun to dream about and in which your generation will know the anguish and the joy of the early settlers.

The Sisters of Loretto of this generation believe in that intellectual-spiritual frontier. Under the leadership of Sister Luke, our Superior General, and Sister Rose Maureen, our Provincial, the General Council of the Sisters of Loretto has voted to request from the chancery canonical permission to transfer the ownership of Webster College to a self-perpetuating Board of Directors. We who are members of both the community of the Sisters of Loretto and at the same time are members of the administration, faculty, student body, and staff of the wider community that is Webster College are proud of our family which has come to believe so deeply in the maturity of that which it has generated. If the canonical approval comes through, the Sisters, along with dedicated laymen, will remain committed to the Webster College we all love. Convinced of the power of religious presence as distinct from the power of religious control, we wish to demonstrate to an open and opening world, *and to ourselves,* that the vital force of faith can live and mature in a diverse and dynamic society.

A number of highly competent men and women in various parts of the country have indicated a willingness to serve on the Board of Directors if and when legal ownership becomes vested in such a board. All are persons who have come to believe in the *fact* that is today's Webster College and in the potential that lies within that fact.

The first commission to try to effect this new incorporation was given me by the General Council of the Sisters of Loretto early last February. Shortly thereafter, Sister Luke and Sister Rose Maureen shared this information first with the Sisters here at Webster and then with the congregation at large. In early spring, we met with the faculty to communicate to them the direction we wanted to take. We have tried, to this point successfully, to keep the matter out of the public press. In these sensitive days garbled versions of requesting canonical approval could be disastrous. However, I felt at this time it was imperative to share with all of you who are the *fact* of Webster College, the vision, the plans, the negotiations of the parent company to make legal and permanent our maturity and independence as a college. I asked and received Sister Rose Maureen's approval to make this public speech to all of you—in the privacy of the college community without reporters or newspaper release. I know that you will hold the information in trust—that you will be prepared for the garbled versions that will be inevitable when the news becomes public.

Suspicion and criticism are, indeed, inevitable. Some healthy skepticism is even desirable. But you and I know that history records not suspicion and criticism or even skepticism, but deeds. By our deeds, they shall know us. If we and the generations that follow us are responsible, compassionate, concerned, magnanimous, and faithful, we will be known as men of faith and we will open faith to and with men to whom it has been heretofore closed by narrowness of vision.

Today, my colleagues, is Founders' Day—for me, for you, for the generations who will remake and refound what we bequeath to them in freedom and in trust.

One hundred and fifty-four years after the event of a log-cabin school on the Kentucky frontier, we thank God for Mary Rhodes and Christina Stuart and Nancy Havern. A century after the covered wagons and open prairies that led to the frontier of the Southwest, we thank God for Mother Praxedes. Fifty-one years after the founding of Webster College, we thank God for Sister Louise Wise.

May we join in a commitment that future generations may thank God for the General Council, the administration, the faculty, the students, and a developing new body of trustees who faced the intellectual-spiritual frontier of 1966 and formed a new and wide community to address itself to a new and wider task. History records. Men *do*. Let us begin.

I   The New Generation

. . . indeed you are the new generation, the new generation to whom we will pass on the courage and the challenge and the possibilities and the potential of our world.

—June 6, 1965

*Who are the persons, the human persons, the finite
persons, that we respect most? They are the ones
who love and trust power into us.*

Baccalaureate Address
Webster High School
June 6, 1965

"I have not come to destroy, but to fulfill. I have come that
you may have life and have it more abundantly." It is with
this spirit that I have come to you tonight to share the joyous
grace of this evening. It is such a joy for me because twenty-
one years ago, in 1944, I was seventeen and sitting in a white
dress in a church at a baccalaureate service. I am told that we
commonly contemplate or calculate a generation at twenty-
one years. And so, indeed, you are the new generation. The
new generation to whom we will pass on the courage and the
challenge and the possibilities and the potential of our world.
I am a firm believer in the new generation and in the ensuing
generations, because I am a devotee of the evolution of man
and of the future of man. I believe that we live in the babyhood of mankind, with maybe a million or two million years

behind us, and perhaps with hundreds of millions of years before us.

On the night that I sat in a white dress in a church in a little provincial town in northern Illinois the world had not learned about the ecumenical world of search. The world had not yet produced an open society: the open society that could bring the Cardinal of my church to this pulpit two nights ago to participate in the graduation of Eden Seminary and to receive an honorary doctorate of divinity from "another" church: the same ecumenical world of search that could let me, a Catholic nun as a citizen of Webster Groves, share with you, at this pulpit, in a graduating point in your lives. This point in time was caused by all kinds of things: by technological advances which allowed our communication system to open up the world; technological advances, all of which have happened since that night just twenty-one years ago, about three years before you were born, when I sat in your place. Since that time television is an actuality, and so we know that at this moment we can watch as a man walks above and across the United States in less than twelve minutes. But we can also watch the emerging nations come into being. We can watch as we perpetrate, sometimes, terrible hypocrisies on the democratic spirit in Selma, Alabama; in Detroit, Michigan; and perhaps in the city of St. Louis. No longer is it possible for a man to live in isolation. Perhaps this is the greatest gift Almighty God has ever given us—the great potency that he has given to your generation, who, at the beginning of your adult lives, live in a world in which it is impossible to be provincial, in which it may be impossible for you to be egoistic because the world is opened up. If, indeed, you are going to be fulfilled; if, indeed, you are going to live full lives, then you must live inside the open society and find your own fulfillment in the fulfillment of all men.

It is a joyous grace for me to be here tonight because it is the feast of Pentecost, a most appropriate feast, I think; a feast that is a "generated" feast, generated by the Jewish religion in the Old Testament, bequeathed to those of us in the New Testament, yet still shared with those who profess the Old Testament. The feast of Pentecost, which to the Jews was the consummation of the harvest, was the conclusion of the covenant between God and the people. The feast of Pentecost for Christians is the consummation of the Incarnation, of the Redemption; the time in which God, indeed, passed on his life to the future of man. I hope it is not amiss to compare it to a line I think all of us love from the Kennedy inaugural address. John Kennedy said on that cold winter morning, "The torch is passed to a new generation and it shall not be passed back." I am sure that all of us, wherever we were on that bleak November afternoon, heard the echo of that phrase, heard it in agony. And yet it remains true. John Kennedy that day did not speak just for himself. He spoke for a moment in the evolution of man—a moment when we could not turn back to isolationism, not national isolationism or state isolationism or city isolationism, or perhaps even international isolationism. We cannot turn back to socioeconomic strata, to political strata, to religious strata, to philosophic strata. And in this passing of the torch to a new generation, I firmly believe, we are really beginning to discover the meaning of Christianity. The life of Christ, on Pentecost, became the Christian life. It became the Christian life for the ongoing generation through the indwelling of the spirit of God.

I think all of the Christian religions have some notion, some understanding, some concept of what we commonly call grace. Grace, in my estimation, is nothing but the indwelling of the life and love of God, the communion of love between human beings. You were loved into being by two people who are sitting behind you; loved into physical being by an act of love which brought you life; sustained in being, qualified in being, able to grow in being and life because they sustained you with their love for each other, and with their love for you. No two people in the world are more important to me than my parents, now fifty-one years married, the couple who sat behind me on my baccalaureate night, the persons who are more responsible than any other persons for the generation and the sustenance and the nurturing of my own life.

Yet you are twenty-one years better off than I am; you are forty years better off than some of the people sitting behind you. The very worth of our lives is dependent upon your outstripping us. Your teachers, who probably sit behind you, too, are depending on your being better mathematicians, better scientists, better philosophers, better students of literature than they are. If they give you only that which they had, then that which they had is a static gift and not a dynamic power. But if they give you the spirit of the frontiersman, the intellectual frontiersman, the spiritual frontiersman, they give you the power to go on, pushing back the future and making for all men a more perfect and perfectable life.

The Christ said, "A new commandment I give unto you: that you love one another as I have loved you." And he said, "By this shall all men know that you are my disciples: if you have love for one another." Yet when I was your age and until within this present decade, even the parking lot between Webster College and the Episcopal church was its own Berlin wall. But somehow, in this last decade, in this last magnificent decade, the psychological spiritual Berlin walls have begun to come down; and we, at last, seem to be free to realize that we live in a contemplative *world,* in a contemplative *life,* in a life where each of us is intellectually and spiritually humble, where we realize, as I sometimes realize, that we are something like .000000000 . . . 000001 of the human race. If you wake up tonight, as I sometimes wake up, and you realize that that is all you are, it can be a frightening kind of experience. You see, you are only one of hundreds of millions that populate the earth now, and you are only one generation of, I believe, hundreds of thousands of generations that are yet to come. And so if you put your value on a quantitative basis, you have sold yourself terribly short. But, if you put your value on a power basis, on a generative basis, on a spiritual-formation basis, indeed, each of us may have a tremendous impact and force for the future of man.

I can see no other way for a man or a woman to invest his life than to invest his life in the future. Only by investing his life in the future will his present investment yield joyous dividends.

What did Christ mean when he said "as I have loved you"? Let's look not at a single action, but at the pattern of his actions. Let's look only at the Gospel, the great scripture which the Protestant church is letting us get back to after we were not so smart! We look at the scripture together as one looks at a biography—not to look at a series of words, but only, somehow, to discover the spirit of a man. We look at scripture to discover the spirit of Christ; to try, somehow, to fathom the wonderment of the embryonic seed that he was leaving there for you and me to bring to fruition a little more in each generation. Look at the Christ in the way he treated Peter, and Matthew, and Zacchaeus up in the tree, and John, and Magdalene, the woman taken in adultery—a wonderful polyglot of persons: Matthew the tax-gatherer; Mary Magdalene, whom he wasn't supposed to be seen with (because *you* know the religious people are always awfully hard on you if you are seen with the wrong person), the woman taken in adultery, whom all the religious people wanted to condemn, the religious people who wanted to catch the Christ in a dilemma so that he would either be unjust to the law or betray his great, gentle, compassionate spirit. We know that story—in my estimation, the greatest of all Gospel stories —when they said, "Will you stone her?" And he said, "Let him who is without sin cast the first stone." And then after that great fictional *tour de force* when he wrote in the sand (and Christ was a great fiction writer because he did not "blow" his novel by letting us know what he wrote), the people went away—beginning with the oldest. The woman came to him, and he said, "Has no man condemned thee?" And she said, "No man, Lord." And he said, "Then neither will I condemn thee. Go, and sin no more."

There is, I think, a profound implication in that story which we might miss. Not only did he not condemn her, but he created a society in which she could not be condemned. He simply used the wits of his imagination as well as the compassion of his heart to outwit the hypocritical-judgment people, who were the only group in the Gospel that Christ was ever severe with. The Gospel calls them the "Pharisees," and every generation has had its share. The Pharisee always thinks that the religious spirit is summed up in judging other persons. The Pharisee is mirrored today in the well-meaning suburban woman who *tch-tchs* over coffee about those awful women of the streets in the slums. The Pharisee in our society is represented by the family that rejects its child the first time the child does something which casts disfavor on the family. The Pharisee might be a Roman Catholic nun who, in the terms that were used to describe the Jansenistic nuns a couple of centuries ago, might be as pure as an angel and as proud and cold as a devil. This is the kind of Pharisaism which feeds upon the lack of compassion for other human beings. There is nothing in the Gospel that shows anything but compassion,

except for the Pharisees to whom Christ was not compassionate: the Pharisees whom he drove out of the temple for col-
lecting from persons on religious grounds and on *unjust*
grounds; the Pharisees who tried to trap him on hypocritical
grounds. On the weak, on the loving, on the warm, he exer-
cised nothing but compassion, nothing but warmth and trust
and a magnetic personality. We are told that all of the persons, all of the apostles followed him—left what they had to
do and followed him—because he had a magnetic personality.
And then we look at what we have done to him, what we
have done to him in those simpering, feminine, unbelievable
pictures that no man would ever look at; at what we have
done to him in making him a taskmaster who is just waiting
for us to make one mistake!

Who are the persons, the human persons, the finite persons,
who love us most? Who are the persons, the human persons,
the finite persons, that we respect most? They are the ones
who love and trust power into us. They are the ones who, like
the father, are waiting up at the top of the hill for the prodi-
gal to come back—waiting, waiting and watching to make
him welcome when he does come back. Not the brother, not
the older brother who defended his religious dignity as being
better than that of the younger son who went out and fed
among the swine. The father is the image, the image of God.

Twenty-one years from now somewhere in a church in the
United States, or somewhere in a church in the world, or
maybe somewhere in a church on the moon, there may be
another set of young women in white and young men in ties,
and a few of them may be your sons and daughters. At the
rate of early marriage in this country, I think I could make a
prediction that a few of them will be your sons and daughters. The decisions you make tonight, the decisions you make
tomorrow, the decisions you make in the next four years in

college or in business will help to shape the future of those persons.

By what kind of criteria will you make your decision? I would like to suggest one great fountain to which we can go back and back and try to fathom what Christ meant by his words. The fountain is the Sermon on the Mount in which he said "Blessed are the poor in spirit." He did not mean those who gave away their riches, necessarily. I have known all too many persons who gave away plenty and have no empathy for their brothers! He meant those who share the lot of their brothers, those who share the lot of mankind: those who know what it is to feel the agony of a woman living on aid-to-dependent-children payments; someone who knows the agony of a person in a ghetto area who lacks the knowledge to cope with the high interest rates being perpetrated on him; some-one who knows what it is like, or what it used to be like, to be kept out of a restaurant in Webster Groves because of the color of his skin; someone who knows what it is like not to be able to buy a house. This is the challenge of your generation; but do not condemn your parents. Your parents have made magnificent strides with what they had at seventeen, it seems to me. The generation of those who are now forty-five or fifty are making heroic efforts to meet, for instance, the integration crisis. But they're giving to you the artifact of 1965. And they're giving to you the power at seventeen really to invent a future in which the Constitution and the Declaration of Independence are at last honest, in which Christianity is at last honest. Those who are poor in spirit share the lot of their brothers. In the words of Atticus in that lovely novel, *To Kill a Mockingbird,* "You never really understand a person until you climb into his skin and walk around in it." Unless I can somehow make some effort to get inside the skin of a seventeen-year-old boy, unless you can somehow make an effort to get inside the skin (if you can get through the robes) of a thirty-eight-year-old nun, we don't know each other, and we have nothing to share; we have nothing to communicate; we have no common ground by which you and I can seek the future, the future of this life and the future of eternity.

And he said "Blessed are the meek." He did not mean blessed are those who are trampled on; but he meant blessed are the sensitive, blessed are those who are not egoistic, blessed are those who are using the power of their personality, the power of their character, the power of their talent to go out and be sensitive to mankind everywhere. He said "Blessed are those who mourn." I think he meant those who give to each other mutual comfort, mutual comfort when the going is tough, mutual comfort when you lose your first child, mutual comfort when your husband loses his job, mutual comfort when you do not know what to do in modern society. I hope not mutual comfort when you have to face a war, a war of the consequences that we were facing when I sat in that white dress. I hope we never have to face that again. You have the power. You, the voting citizenry, but much more important, you the *communicating* citizenry who give the ideas to each other. You have the power mutually to make each other strong, and that is what "comfort" means.

"Blessed are those who hunger and thirst after justice." Blessed are those. Nothing is more important to the United States of America than due process of law—nothing. Even if we suffer individually, the future of our children lies in our being loyal to every man having a right to the due process of law, to a man not being condemned without sufficient evidence. You must hunger and thirst after justice in the sense of the due process of law, because no individual is saved any more by a benevolent, patronizing spirit. That kind of charity is no longer effective. We live in a complex society; we live in an international society; and only the due process of law can save us. I think the due process of law, as we are trying to find it today, was deep in the embryonic germ of Christ's words when he said "Blessed are those who hunger and thirst after justice."

"Blessed are the merciful"—blessed are those who have compassion; blessed are those who do not judge; blessed are those who suffer with other persons, who "compassionate" with other persons. The greatest people I have ever known have always had a deep reservoir of compassion—the deep reservoir that not only envelops you in their arms but also makes you *know* that you will be enveloped in their arms, makes you *know* that you will not be held apart out of coldness.

"Blessed are the clean of heart." That is a tough one. Our puritan culture, our Jansenistic culture, has given us one kind of focus on this one. So you get all kinds of lectures on being careful when you are in a parked car! I shall leave those lectures and those discussions to another time and another person, and I am sure they are things that should be discussed. But I want to look at the clean of heart in a little different way tonight. I want to look at the clean of heart as the "transparent of heart." The transparent of heart whom God can look at and see no jealousy, no meanness, nothing is trying to beat somebody else out of what is his due, nothing that is trying to hide under a hypocritical spirit, some selfish, egoistic, non-magnanimous spirit. It seems to me that if we are transparent in that sense, we will discover what love is. One generation might even communicate to you the wonder of love, the fantastic wonder of love. And if you find the fantastic wonder of love (you will find your way to finding it), then no one will have to lecture about the parked cars.

"Blessed are the peacemakers." Blessed are those who today

believe in passive resistance. Blessed are the Martin Luther Kings, not because they are infallible, not because they are not making mistakes, but because they know they are finite human beings who are trying, inch by inch, to make a better world, not by war, but by passive resistance. Some brilliant scientist friends of mine firmly believe that Martin Luther King's passive resistance movement is the most important movement for modern man; not only to solve the problem of integration, though that be important to be solved, but because they are inventing the key to our being able to live in a complex world. Of course, we cannot afford atomic warfare. Dr. Jerome B. Wiesner, President Kennedy's science advisor, told me on the night of signing the Test Ban Treaty, a treaty that he had sweat and bled and worked for, "Sister Jacqueline, all we did today was to take a baby step. It really doesn't amount to anything. But we have to take that baby step and we have to see whether we can make that baby step hold and if we can make that baby step hold, we can take another baby step and another baby step and another and only in this way do we have a chance for disarmament." Only in this way do we have a chance for disarmament. Only so does that little baby who is crying back there have a chance to live in a world in which there is love. Disarmament is a terribly dangerous endeavor, terribly dangerous. But unless we will try, unless we live in trust and adventure and love instead of fear, we will pile up stock arms; we will have great turmoil between the races. But unless we try we will not discover (by trial and error, by hurt and success) how to become *really* the children of God.

Last of all he said, "Blessed are those who suffer persecution for justice's sake." Again, I think, some of the religionists in the Protestant and the Catholic faith did not read the sentence far enough. Some of them only read it "Blessed are those that suffer." They somehow got mixed up and thought that to suffer was of itself good. To deny oneself something was of itself good. I no longer believe that. I believe that the only good is fulfillment; the only good is progress. But many times we have to suffer in order to get progress. I am sure no astronaut enjoys being strapped into that seat. He gets strapped into that seat in order to orbit; but he would be a blasted fool if he gets strapped into the seat in order to be virtuous. Our day no longer needs the self-imposed mortification—the self-implied mortifications by which we live with our egoistic tiny consciences and then do not respond to a world. Our world, your world, the world that you have a longer chance at than I have—that world leads you sometimes to suffer persecution for justice's sake; for justice's sake on all accounts: for religious justice, social justice, economic justice, personal justice. It needs you, and sometimes you will have to be the seed that goes into the ground and dies. But remember what He said: "The seed that goes into the ground and dies in order that it may bring forth life."

We have come full circle. "I have not come to destroy, but to fulfill. I have come that you may have life and have it more abundantly." And if, indeed, I get to run to and through my grave, I hope—somehow—in that heaven I really know very little about, perhaps nothing about, He will let me look down, in something like 2020, when you still have a chance to be alive, and I can watch you outstrip everything that I and my generation managed to do. May you lead joyous, grace-filled lives knowing that you are given life, loved and trusted into more being by your mother and father, by your ministers, by your teachers, even by a Roman Catholic nun.

I ought to go where nobody else will go.
I ought to look at what nobody else will look at.

Convocation Address
Texas Southern University
October 6, 1964

I come to rejoice with you that you are members of a university which is only just beginning to be in the making. I think perhaps that is your greatest privilege, that you are members of a university that is just being born.

You see, I think the most precious privilege an individual can have is to share in the making of great enterprises.

I am never interested in joining in a project that is already made. It is the frontiers that are important. It is the frontiers that are capable of shaping great people. The frontiers are filled with challenge; the frontiers are filled with the process of doing things; of asking hard and long questions of reality; and of helping together with many other people to find approximating answers—which will always be finite—and moving on to the new questions which we are able to ask at any given time.

We hear a lot today about a word that worries me a good bit, the word *status*. We read much in popular magazines about "status-seeking," about the preoccupation we all have with status.

I am worried about the word *status* because the word in itself means stationary—a position, a fixed position. And I happen to believe that fixed positions and static conditions are the most devastating things that can happen to the human person.

It is not nearly so important where I stand as it is where I look, where I seek, where I question; how I look, how I seek, how I question.

It is where I am going that is important, not where I am. It is what I can possibly try to do with my life that is important, not what I am at this precise moment.

I am sure that each of you has heard people talk about vested interest. When a company has a vested interest it is in danger of not looking with anything like clarity at a peculiar problem. When a social group has a vested interest it has a very hard time looking at an open question. When a religious group has a vested interest, the members have very great difficulty in looking at an open question. When an educational group has a vested interest, or an academic discipline has a vested interest, or a youth group has a vested interest, in so much as that group hangs on tenaciously to that vested interest it is prohibited; it is held back from running ahead to ask the great new question.

There is a company in my area for which I have a great respect—Monsanto Chemical Company. It has its executive offices in the St. Louis area. But more important than the offices of the administrative team is the great center for research and development. On a campus which is much like an educational campus is a research and development center valued at multi-multimillions in which the research scientists invent new things all the time.

The Monsanto people are totally aware that what is being invented in that laboratory will be for the most part thrown away. They are aware that about 90 per cent of what they will try will prove to be invalid, but that 10 per cent of what they try will be the making of Monsanto for the next decade, will be the reason that Monsanto will remain a leader in the generations of science research.

And so they pour multimillion dollars into that enterprise. They give to their scientists the best kind of working conditions and they give to them something much more important than good working conditions—they give them the high degree of freedom without which the human mind cannot pursue truth.

I was told recently of statistics which cannot be dislodged from my mind. In 1946, the gross sales of Monsanto Chemical Company were thirty-five million dollars; in 1963, only seventeen years later, the gross sales of Monsanto Chemical Company were one billion three-hundred-fifty million dollars.

How did they do it? They did it by putting together a team of people who would not be trapped by vested interest. They put together a team of people who said the discoveries of today are only the springboard of tomorrow. Along with this, they realized they had to put into their company the principle of power which makes a man not just a technician of this age but an inventor of the age to come. In this sense I have become fascinated by Monsanto and I have been telling my educational colleagues at home and abroad that it is this kind of ambition, this kind of gambling spirit, that we must put back into the educational enterprises.

If the educational enterprise is involved with learning, then it is always involved with the process of invention. The facts

that somebody else found are important to me as a springboard for finding something else. Our physicist colleagues talk
a lot about successive approximations, but this is a term that
ought to belong to all of us. How do we solve a problem in
mathematics? By successive approximation. How do we solve
a problem in science? By successive approximation. How do
we solve a problem in communications? By successive approximation. How do we solve a problem in social theory, or in religion, or in philosophy? By successive approximation.

I heard a very great theologian at the beginning of this
month, a theologian who gives me courage about being a
member of the Roman Catholic Church. He said we must
think of hard problems as a nut, a nut that is very tough to
crack. And, if we realize that the nut is very tough to crack,
we are apt to fall into one of two dangers; either we will
throw the nut away or we will pretend that we have cracked
it. Instead, we must hold that nut and attempt to invent the
implement that will crack the nut because it is what is inside
that really counts.

I hope that my own church and many other Christian
churches at this time are going back to a position of being
intellectually humble. Of recognizing that we indeed have
finite minds; finite, limited minds which are always trying to
make successive approximations about infinite realities.

I remember when I was a little girl on a farm in Illinois,
lying out on the back lawn one night, looking up at the stars
and wondering if there were a God. And, I kept looking and I
kept wondering how far it was, and I kept remembering what
they had told me in religion classes about the fact that I
would go to heaven if I was good and that I was going to
look at God and contemplate God forever, and ever, and ever,
and ever, and ever, and ever. And my little eight-year-old

mind said forever, and ever, and ever, and ever, and ever
—how dull!

All my life that echo kept coming back like the refrain from
a chorale—forever and ever and ever . . . is it really exciting? But in this decade of my life I have decided that indeed
it *is* exciting, because I have begun to find life exciting; exciting because it is difficult, exciting because there is so much to
do. I find myself sometimes going to bed at night and getting up in the morning wondering what I would do if I believed in reincarnation; wondering how I would spend my
life, if I had two lives instead of one, or five lives instead of
one, or ten lives instead of one, and I find all the exciting
things I cannot get to, all the exciting fields I would like to
study, all the stimulating people I might get to talk to if I
only had time; all the hard problems I might be able to
agonize with in order to be able to work toward their solu-
tion. I find myself wishing I had two lives, or ten lives or a
hundred lives or five-hundred lives because life is anything
but dull.

If this is true, then my thirty-eight-year-old mind is much
more able than my eight-year-old mind to think about the
possibility of learning and of approximating what is there in
the forever, and ever, and ever, and ever.

And so, if God is good to me, I hope I will run to my grave
and run through it and go on being a naïve wide-eyed wonder child who is trying to find out something of the wonder of
what is there.

In that sense it seems to me that we need a tremendous
kind of educational evolution in this country. We have too
long supported in our students on every level—in first grade,
in junior high school, in secondary school, and in our colleges
and our graduate schools—an attitude of status-seeking. Of

trying to read the mind of the professor and find out how he wants me to look—what he wants me to say.

I too have played that game, as I am sure you have. If the teacher believed that the classical school of literature was much superior to the romantic school of literature, I could write glorious exams in which the classical school of literature was a much better school than the romantic one. And, if the teacher next door had a penchant for the romantic school, I could wax eloquent about Keats or Shelley. Because all one had to be was a reader of the expectancy of the teacher. This kind of education reinforces status-seeking. Rather than developing exploratory, inquisitive, inquiring, and contemplative people, we are too often forming people who are trying to reach what is expected of them.

If 5 per cent of you in this audience could get really excited about taking chances, could get really excited about being gamblers, you would transform the world in which you live! But inasmuch as you hold on to the crutch of vested interest: inasmuch as you look for social security in the broad sense, you will lose the power to be inventive, courageous people.

If 5 per cent of you could decide you are here to learn, you are here to investigate, to investigate with terrible freedom and terrible responsibility, then it is among those 5 per cent that we will produce the people who for the next generation will continue to transform the face of the United States of America—if you can responsibly decide to be independent, to trust your own nerves.

If you have a little money to invest, you can invest it in the security of a 4½ per cent savings account or in the blue-chip stocks. If I had had a few dollars a few years ago to invest, I wish I had invested it in IBM or Polaroid before IBM and Polaroid were "safe" investments. But much more important than that, if I have only one *life* to live, if I have only one life to spend, and I can only spend it once (and nobody's proved to me yet that there is reincarnation, so I guess I can spend it only once), then I want to look around and see where I can get the most for my spending.

I am sure that if you young women in the audience had thirty or forty dollars and saw hanging on the rods of a dress shop lots and lots of beautiful dresses (if you are like me before I decided to put myself into this habit), you would look up and down that rack and say "I like that one because I look nice in red" or "I like that one because of where I could wear it" or "I like that one because it would serve for more purposes." And so you end with the very real problem of trying to spend your money where you will get most of what you want.

What we do too often when we invest in an education or when we invest our lives—unless things have changed more than I think they have changed—is to cheat ourselves. There are all too many students who look at the list of courses and say "Where can I get least for my money; who is the easy teacher?" instead of saying "I am here to invest my money, or my parents' money, or the state's money, or an aggregate of all, and I am here to invest something much more than that. I am here to invest that piece of my life—I am nineteen and I'll never be nineteen again. Where can I develop the most power; whose class can I get into that will challenge me most?" Too often a student will look at that list and say "That's an easy breeze; I shall go through it that way." I suggest that if students ever wake up to this phenomenon they will never let us cheat them. If they have weak teachers, teachers who let them off easy, teachers who allow them to do next to nothing for their investment, instead of passing on the word "sign up for that class," they will let that class lie empty with open seats because it simply is not worth it. As an administrator, I wish students would begin to do this, for then I would tell that faculty member that I no longer need him for he too has to earn his way. If we begin to think in this fashion, we will think of education as power. We will think of education as the power to lift reality.

Perhaps you have heard one of the many many stories that have been told about the late President of the United States, John Fitzgerald Kennedy. It is told that he was asked why he wanted to be President of the United States, when he seemingly had so much. And he said very simply that he looked around his world and tried to decide where he could exercise most leverage on the world. And he said after a long look that he decided that the place a man could exercise more leverage on the world than in any other position was as the President of the United States and so he decided to try for it.

This, I think, embodies the rare paradox of ambition and humility: ambition to say "Where can I make the great impact? Where can I be most powerful?" and then to take the awfully humble position of saying "I will *try* for it!"

My friends, I will tell you from my little experience, and I am sure anyone else who happens to be a little older than you will tell you from his experience, that when you decide to try, you expose yourself to terrible hurt. You expose yourself to failure, and failure is bitter in the mouth. Most people who fail will say that whether it be failure in getting a good grade in class or whether it be failure in working a mathematics problem; whether it be failure in getting an elective office that one tries for; whether it be failure in simply living a good life, failure is bitter in the mouth. Ninety per cent of the people, perhaps more than that, quit and put around themselves a defensive, protective kind of armor because the taste of failure is bitter indeed.

But some 10 per cent of the people more or less decide that

the taste of failure is not nearly so expensive, that it is worth the wonder of succeeding, of experiencing the wonder of being productive to oneself and to one's world. When we think in this way, I think, we become ambitious but not ruthlessly ambitious; we become ambitious in the sense of wanting to use ourselves as a power instrument for all people.

A television correspondent recently told me a lovely little anecdote that was not published about the late President which I think balances the other one.

When John Kennedy called a press conference one Sunday afternoon in the White House, a CBS cub reporter made a terrible mistake. You are always supposed to be on instant call if you are on White House duty, and the young reporter forgot to tell them where he would be. Kennedy called the press conference. The reporters came and the news broadcast was video-taped. And, as the poor cub reporter ran into the White House, the ABC and NBC reporters were going out and the film was finished.

The cub reporter went in and moaned to Pierre Salinger: "I'm finished; do you realize, I'm finished! No man makes a mistake like this! Not only do I lose this job but I'll lose any possible job in television in the future." As Salinger was trying to console him, the President of the United States strode into the room and asked what the matter was.

The young reporter, still in emotional anguish, poured out his story to the President of the United States. And John Kennedy smiled and said "Suppose we do it again." Then, with no one knowing it, the President gave the press interview completely and exactly as he had done it a few minutes earlier, and no one on the news broadcast that night knew the difference. He did it to save one cub reporter who was trying.

This, I think, is what we are trying to get out of ourselves. First of all, that when you are trying to communicate to a society, you become terribly ambitious; you aim for the highest kind of power, because power is the only thing that you can work with—personal power that is inside you. But you must also become empathic and compassionate with people everywhere else, for people who do not understand what you understand, for people who do not understand you.

I am today terribly excited to be a Roman Catholic Sister in the United States of America because I am in the toughest kind of position. I live in a conventional world where people expect me to live inside a cloister, where people expect me not to know quite what the reality of life is all about. I live inside a church that people think of as being still quite authoritarian and autocratic. Yet a great old man named John XXIII tried to change things. I live inside an educational bailiwick where people expect us to be thoroughly conservative because education has been conservative. And yet precisely because I live inside all of these, I have the great advantage of trying to invent my way out of it: the great advantage of trying to lift the window and give myself first of all the opportunity to see another world.

And so today I am ready to say, at the price of being called a heretic, that the persons who have most made me understand my Christian faith are my atheist friends. The persons who have most made me plumb the depths of my Christian faith are my atheist friends, because they have made me try to find out who I am. But, I have also made them try to find out who they are. In so doing I have become a more powerful person. And so I am no longer concerned, I am no longer willing that anyone of us allow ourselves to work in a ghetto or a province or a parochial kind of atmosphere. Inasmuch as we do not look out at the wider world; inasmuch as we do not go out to the wider world; inasmuch as we live in any kind of provincial atmosphere, we are lost. And we rob the outer world of our kind of contribution.

Young Negroes I think, are perhaps the one group that has even greater privileges and greater challenges than I. If I had a reincarnated life to live, I would love to be one of those students sitting about in the seventh row. I would love to be you, because the challenge ahead of you is so hard, and the challenge ahead of you is so exciting, and you must break down the barriers of all those people, all those stupid people who do not understand.

But you will break down the barriers only if you love those who do not understand; you will break down the barriers only if you are empathic and sympathetic to them. You have got to go 90 per cent of the way, just as I, as a Roman Catholic Sister, have to go 90 per cent of the way, because they need you desperately.

Some of the young students in my college may have John Birch fathers, and some of them need you desperately if they are not to shrink into the kind of wizened raisins who can live in only one kind of society.

I would love to see the day when we could bring some of your faculty to our institution and some of ours here. I would love to have the chance to teach in this kind of institution. I think this is where Roman Catholic sisters are going, because I think the day of the segregated Catholic institution is on its way out. We must live in a larger world; we must interact with the larger world; but each of us has to become powerful to do that, and that is the meaning of education.

In that sense the college course, whether it be a course in anthropology or physics or philosophy, or English or mathematics, or whatever it may be—the course that torments you, the course that troubles you, the course that makes you keep asking questions when you go to bed at night and when you get up in the morning—that's the course that's worth the investment. The teacher who troubles you, the teacher who doesn't give you pat answers and platitudes, is the teacher that will make it impossible for the United States to have a John Birch Society. The extremist positions in any field are positions of indoctrination; they are positions which allow us to take a formula from somebody else and not to question the tough haunting questions—the tough haunting realities.

If a teacher, if a course, if an experience can trouble me, can send me out to know that life is tough but wonderful; then I will see it as an adventure and lead a very, very exciting life.

If I believe in God, if I believe in grace, if I believe that I share at all in the power which is God, then I ought to be the greatest gambler in the history of mankind. I ought to go where nobody else will go. I ought to look at what nobody else will look at.

I have often said to our own students at home that a prostitute ought to be able to be most comfortable with a Roman Catholic sister because it was the Christ who went out to the women of the Pharisees and the women taken in adultery and the woman at the well. It was the Christ who made everybody comfortable except the hypocrites.

This, I think, is the challenge that lies before all of us. To subscribe to an education, to subscribe to an inquiry, to a questioning that will free us to become powerful with that power of our human nature which some of us believe is the grace of God.

This I ask you to share with me; to share with me because it is the most precious thing that we do share.

Unless there are some of you in this audience who will be more powerful than any of us who are sitting on the stage by

1980, all of us who are sitting on the stage are colossal failures. Life is evolutionary, and it is our purpose to communicate to you the power which will make you, with the advancement of the human race, more powerful than those of us who lived before you.

I hope when I am an old lady and running to my grave, someone will tell me, perhaps, that the President of the United States, the man who is lifting the lever of the world, sat in my audience one day in October in Texas.

Only if you and I free this [new] generation from our grasp,
only if we support their lives rather than asking them to support
our egos by letting us live through them, will they be free to
respect and to love us.

Commencement Address
John Burroughs School
June 9, 1967

A few years ago there was an extraordinarily popular television program originating from England called "That Was the Week That Was." I somehow feel that all of us have some feeling that we have just lived through such a week. Even as you engage in the social whirl surrounding this commencement weekend, I am sure many of you are also engaged in a really personal way in a human drama being played out in the Middle East. Now as the world capitals try to sort out the issues that provoked the conflict and the complex political labyrinth surrounding the conflict, all of them and all of us are again a little awed at the sheer communal strength of the Israelis. I do not propose to analyze political issues, much less to make an authoritative value judgment on them. I am not in any way an authority on Middle Eastern problems. However, I do want us to think together about one remark made by James Reston of *The New York Times* in his column originating in Tel Aviv yesterday. Reston, who had been in Cairo at the beginning of the week, made this observation: "The constrast between the spirit of Tel Aviv and the spirit of Cairo just a few days ago is remarkable and must have something to do with the outcome of this war. Cairo was run from the top and was full of misery and hopelessness at the bottom. Tel Aviv is full of lively talk and debate and personal responsibility."

Two summers ago, I spent an all-too-short two-week period in the State of Israel. It remains one of the memorable experiences of my life. As a guest of the Jewish federation, I was the only Roman Catholic and one of four Christians in a group of Jewish people from St. Louis. It was of course a real joy to visit the places that are the very roots of my own religious culture. However, the most important spiritual experiences for me took place in the Hall of the Six Million in Jerusalem (*Yad Vashem*) and on the campus of the Hebrew University in New Jerusalem. As I stood in the simple rotunda of the Six Million and looked at the stark black-and-white signboards "commemorating" each of the Nazi concentration camps with the number of Jews who were slaughtered there written below the name of the place, I experienced as great a physical oppression as I have ever known. Intellectually, I had known the horror of the Nazi massacre of the Jews. Intellectually, I was somewhat aware of the history of Jewish pogroms. But that day in the midst of my Jewish friends in the Hall of the Six Million, the greatest single failure of Western Christianity was bleakly apparent. In the name of what orthodoxy, in the name of what god, could a Western Christian world engage in or permit such inhumanity?

A few days before or after that experience, we stood on a hillside on the campus of the Hebrew University. One could see in the distance the earlier Hebrew University in the Old Jerusalem. The newer one, then less than seventeen years old, was, even in its brick and mortar, an impressive reality. Walking across that campus were not only Israelis but also students from other parts of Asia and of Africa. The Hebrew University was obviously not committed to be a new Jewish ghetto. The buildings of the university were made of a beautiful stone. As I looked a little beyond them to the hillside on which they were built, I noticed first some blocks that had been cut from stone. Then I realized that the building blocks of the new Hebrew University were indeed formed day by day from the very rocks grubbed out of the hillside on which the university was built. Echoing in my memory was that lovely passage from one of the testaments which says simply that the stone which the builders rejected has become the cornerstone. Out of adversity they had forged the future. The rocks that were in their way and had blocked advancement had become the building blocks.

I knew that here was a miracle of vitality that was not part of the somber puritan work ethic that has so often dominated our culture. Neither was this, by some miracle, the honed-out martyrdom of the oppressed who had become cynical. In all fairness, I should also say that I had visited the orthodox quarter with very ambiguous feelings. Here, at least to the eyes of the novice, was a commitment to the past and an entrenchment in a historical artifact, coupled with a conscious determination to ignore the evolutionary drama that was taking place all around them. I had visited, too, some of the Arab quarters within Israel with the same kind of ambiguity.

It seemed to me then as, indeed, it seems to me now, that whether modern Israel would assume its destiny or reject it would depend on how it resolved the tension of whether Israel would be a historic sanctuary in the narrow sense of

Zionism or a germinal center of an evolutionary world which might, indeed, break down the national and ethnic ghetto in investing in the community of man.

On our last night in the country, in a little bistro in Tel Aviv, Teddy Kollek, now the Mayor of Jerusalem, and I had a great conversation shouting over the Israeli combo. A protégé of Ben-Gurion, Kollek is in every way the secular Israeli who is at the same time deeply spiritual. I asked him how he felt about intermarriage. He answered that he was not concerned about it in Israel, since it was obvious that there was enough common cause to hold the people together there. However, he told me that he would be concerned about marriage between Jews and Gentiles in the United States, because he was not sure that there was enough common cause here to hold them together. Naturally, he countered by asking me my own feeling about the question. I answered honestly, I think, by saying that I would rather have my niece, who was then eighteen, marry a Jew or a Hindu or a Presbyterian or a secular humanist who was devoted to the future of man, to the solving of our racial and socioeconomic problems, than I would for her to marry a John Birch Catholic. I remember that his face lightened up and he shouted "My God, woman, you mean that!" And indeed I do. The realization was made even more clear to me about a year later. Following a television program here in St. Louis, I had a conversation with a young rabbi who took me to task for this position. After we had argued for some time, he finally said with real anguish: "I think I simply must admit to you that my seven-year-old daughter came home the other night and said 'Daddy, is it all right if we intertalk?'"

Indeed we must intertalk. We must intertalk across and within ethnic lines, religious lines, socioeconomic lines, cultural and ideological lines. If the God Who is our Father is ever to be the Father of the common family of men, then our smaller human families must be willing to forego the narrow boundaries of their old constituencies.

Tomorrow or next fall, each of you will move on from here. Its seems almost ludicrous to me that we still call these exercises "commencement." No student of today is "going out" into life, whether that new life be in a college community or elsewhere. You live in the middle of life, even if we, your teachers and your parents, sometimes try not to acknowledge it. But you go on from here, a person formed by your parents and your families, formed by your cultural background, formed by your having been a student at John Burroughs. And each of these is at the same time a power to motivate your future growth and an obstacle to that growth. Our rootedness in a family, in a culture, in an educational style, is always the vital principle of new growth. But we must, at the same time, realize that the necessary finiteness, the necessary limitedness, of each of these pasts provides its own kind of blinders for our looking at the future. The best families, the best schools, the best corporations of every age are always in danger that they will not be the best of the next age, precisely because their vested interest is so great. If one's *status quo* is better than most, one is always prone to be a defender of the general *status quo* that protects one's personal *status quo*.

I know enough about some of the recent graduates of John Burroughs to realize that they are caught up in this realization. Once, the kind of student graduating at this exercise in this place would have seen his responsibility for the future as a beneficent elitist who must serve the less fortunate members of our population. No longer is this, I believe, a viable position. Man at the present time is struggling away from any stratified notion of an elitist society.

Americans once quite rightly perhaps took pride in producing the Horatio Algers who pulled themselves up by their bootstraps and broke the barriers of socioeconomic stratifications. American folklore is full of examples of log cabin-to-White House odysseys. Such examples were a continuing reassurance that it was possible to gain entry and be absorbed by the upper middle class of society.

But the struggle we are both watching and inevitably involved in today is not so much any more an attempt to achieve assimilation within a conventionally acceptable social stratum, either in this nation or in the world community. It may be just beginning to dawn on my generation that Western civilization and the nineteenth-century American dream were important signposts on the road of human evolution. Your generation in Missouri, in Poland, in Nigeria, in Israel, and in Russia will respect the signposts only if they point to an open road and to new worlds where new roads must carry new traffic and new traffic patterns. The tribal culture of affluent St. Louis suburbs gave life and direction to most of you. The tribal culture of an Illinois farm community gave life and direction to me. But if we rely on the security of those somewhat closed cultures to give the primary continuing meaning to our lives, then we abdicate the opportunity and the responsibility to play any meaningful role in giving new meaning to tomorrow.

In their business and professional lives, most of your parents believe and operate pragmatically on an evolutionary principle of producing products which make yesterday's products obsolete. Often, in the process, they almost transform the very companies that produce the products. The corner grocery becomes Kroger's or A&P; the village cobbler becomes Brown or International Shoe; a small aircraft company becomes McDonnell-Douglas; a small chemical company becomes international Monsanto and erases the limiting "Chemical" from its name.

Perhaps the rugged individualists, the venturesome captains of business and industry and of the professions, many of whom were your parents and grandparents, were so involved in building a new industrial and technological society that they welcomed the sanctuary and familiarity of the more stable communities provided by clubs and churches, by fraternities and the right schools.

Tonight, I want to suggest that their venturesomeness in research in technology has produced a world which demands the same kind of venturesomeness in research in its social, fraternal, religious, and educational structures. The great leveling force of Kroger's and Brown Shoe, of McDonnell and Monsanto has destroyed the tribal and feudal world of earlier elitist societies.

Reflective men today are preoccupied with the question of how to preserve and create initiative in what they see as social-welfare states. Many of you in this audience are concerned about "giveaway" education for the masses even as you carefully provide trust funds for your children and grandchildren to insure their social welfare at Princeton or Wellesley in the future. In affluent families, mutual love and support is the only effective goad to individual responsibility and human initiative. Both the Rockefeller and Kennedy families are interesting examples of security and affluence breeding and nurturing social concern, perhaps even social revolution. Only if you and I free this generation from our grasp, only if we *support their lives* rather than asking them to *support our egos* by letting us live through them, will they be free to respect and to love us. Whether we free them or not, I predict that many of them will free themselves. They will become the rugged individualists of the late twentieth century who will go on experimenting with our social, fraternal, religious, and educational structures. If they are as successful in their generation as many of you were in yours, the exclusive clubs, the elitist civic groups, churches, and schools of today will seem in the retrospection of 2000 like the corner grocery, the cobbler's shop, the small chemical or aircraft factory of the early part of the century. Solid citizens—mature, seasoned, rooted—are rightly proud of today's achievements, and understandably concerned about the transformation for which we will not be the architects. Human evolution is the wondrous process of continuous physical generation. May we of this generation have the wisdom, the humility, and the courage to embrace, to foster, to enable that kind of generation in the world community that is the human family. Tribal cultures die out or become remnants of society. The strains that converge and become new species both make and participate in the future. All that John Burroughs is and represents is and has been the best of one kind of tribal world. The life force of John Burroughs for these graduates and for John Burroughs as an institution will be judged, I submit, in the future on how successfully these graduates and the institution become participants in inventing new social structures which will make today's Burroughs obsolete. I have the greatest faith that as you move on to college and make life difficult for me and my university colleagues, for your parents, and for government officials, you will be at the same time making life richer for your children's children, who will then make life difficult for you.

*. . . any institution is only as great as the initiative
and highly personal involvement, the creative
responsibility of each of the individuals in it.*

Peace Corps Address
Washington, D.C.
March 1965

There has been a great deal of discussion in regard to the
Peace Corps and higher education, about whether the focus of
attention and inquiry should center itself on what the individual Peace Corps volunteer could do inside the college or university or whether the focus should rather be put on what the
total Peace Corps learning experience had to say to "learning
about learning" in the United States of America, in our com-
plicated and sometimes very very rigid college and university
structure.

Peace Corps volunteers, for the most part, seem to see their
personal experiences as a magnificent opportunity to discover
their own identity and autonomy in their specific tasks
abroad. As one girl put it, "To impose upon myself my own
constraints, to decide how much I could demand and claim."
And in the claiming she often demanded less. It was for many

PCVs the first intense opportunity to structure their own experience, to integrate their developing knowledge and developing inquiries, as naïve researchers in an alien laboratory. What a terrible kind of corrective to the whole formal process of education if we look square in the face the thought that those of you who have been through twelve and fourteen and sixteen and eighteen years of formal education could still say that *this* was your first opportunity to structure your own inquiry and learning! At the basic level of their own projects they were permitted, even constrained, by their environmental conditions, to learn to learn, to ask questions, to make decisions, to evaluate developments, and to modify their own decisions. They were often frustrated by communication blocks on regional and national levels, but their basic personal involvement was an intense learning experience for which they were personally responsible.

They return to their now somewhat alien complex of higher education in the United States asking of themselves and of the universities: What is knowledge for? What is my obligation once I have acquired knowledge or as I am seeking it? Some are convinced that the personal acquisition of knowledge is for the service of mankind, mankind in the international community.

The communications problem between the PCVs, the regional professionals, and Peace Corps, Washington, indicate to most a need for a definition of limits of freedom and responsibility, with real and effective systems for communication and feedback. Perhaps the feedback issue is most critical of all. In this sense the Peace Corps, admittedly the most democratic of the government agencies, and, in the opinion of most of us, more democratic than most highly stratified institutions of higher education, has much to share with higher education as it, the Peace Corps, continues to learn to learn the art of this kind of communication and feedback in the necessarily growing complexity of any developing institution.

Recent events at Berkeley and elsewhere point up the imperative need of this kind of dialogue—trilogue, multilogue. Communication, the sharing in a common task, is sought by the PCVs and by all concerned students and faculty. Students, faculty, and administrators are at least beginning to work together to design courses, living conditions, and environment that are relevant to the world at large; to define major goals and ways to work toward these; to create, within the universities and outside the universities, laboratories for volunteer involvement.

There is a generally shared conviction that the Peace Corps learning experience shouts out that knowledge is not an accumulation of facts or a demonstration of Ph.D. expertise, but a deepening of insight and power, to "synthesize" in new situations whether they be abroad or next door. In this sense, the good learning experience, PCV or otherwise, liberates a man or a woman to unify knowledge by intense involvement in a deep experience rather than by surface extension of superficial facts. Experiential learning has no real substitute. The college and university campus has room and urgent need for vitality in students and faculty, whether you be twenty-five-year-old learners or fifty-five-year-old learners, those who will probe, who go about changing, modifying *their* environment in *their* way.

We are aware of the threat involved to the institutions, to the persons within the institutions, by intensifying this kind of responsible innovation. The degree of rigidity of closure to innovation is often in proportion to the threat to the individual person or the vested interest of the institution. However, the degree of effectiveness of the sometimes chaotic interchange may be reflected in the statement of a Midwest college president who stated at this conference his realization of the imperative of increasing his risk involvement, of venturing forth in his institution to do some new things strangely. In this sense, conference discussion groups may be models for college and university seminars where learners, some of them called students, some of them called professors, some of them called administrators, but learners all, go on probing together the potential of the university, of the local and world community, of the future of man.

I would like to say that I come to you as a person who, at I hope young middle age, lives within a complex of rigid institutions, one called a religious order, one called the Roman Catholic Church, one called the establishment of higher education. I live within it lyrically at age thirty-eight, with my eyes wide open, saying that I want only to be a *worldly* nun, because the world is the only place in which I can operate, knowing that I have to learn the tactics of the religious order, knowing that I have to learn the tactics of the Roman Catholic Church, knowing that I have to learn the tactics of the world community. Precisely because I love all three, I am committed to be responsibly important in the evolution of these three institutions and of every other institution that concerns the human condition. In this sense the Peace Corps is, for some of us, from the perspective of our own institutions, a ray of new hope. We are saying within our institutions not only by word but also by deed that any institution is only as great as the initiative and highly personal involvement, the creative responsibility, of each of the individuals within it. Each institution must offer not only its own vested-interest kind of contribution, but also the personal investment of its people in the great, great open society with all its needs.

The democratic world is always in . . . danger, because
freedom of speech implies the freedom not to speak.

Convocation Address
Webster College
September 15, 1965

A few minutes ago, Mrs. Stanard, Director of our Public Information Bureau, told me that she had had a call from the St. Louis *Globe Democrat* asking her "Did you not give us the title of Sister Jacqueline's speech as 'Voice and the College Community?'" When Mrs. Stanard said she had, they replied "Well, it just went out on the AP wire as 'Vice and the College Community.'" The latest report is that they stopped the wire, but in case I am burned at the stake tonight or you are burned at the stake for me, know that this is indeed the story of our lives.

I do want to speak with you today about Voice and the College Community. Some of you know that during the past two weeks Sister Mary Rhodes and I shared in the formation of what I am going to call a new community. It was a seminar on "Innovation in Undergraduate Education," held at

Tufts University and shared in by some forty people from across the country from various types of colleges and universities and from many disciplines, ranging from mathematics and physics to writing and political science. It was a community caught up in ideas so pregnant that they must surely take existence in action. One such idea originating with a novelist-playwright, John Hawkes, whom we came to love, fascinated first the section in literary art and then began to infuse the conference as a whole. Mr. Hawkes, a professor of writing at Brown University—but, most important, a writer himself—is thought by many to be one of the most promising young novelists of our time. He did miserably in Freshman English at Harvard, dropped out of college, and returned after the war. Now, some fifteen years later, under a Ford Foundation grant, he has just finished a sabbatical year working with the San Francisco Playhouse. This was his first real involvement in theater after several years of writing novels. He has come out of the experience convinced that the central force of all effective communication—in written or spoken form—is the finding and the developing of a personal voice.

Let me repeat for you an anecdote I think is significant. Hawkes watched a very good actor at Stanford working with a young student trying to read a Shakespearean lyric. The lyric, in the reading, was a collection of empty words. Then the actor asked the student to read it to another actor—to assume that this actor was in great grief and to give him the pure beauty of the lyric as a gift. There was no phony attempt to match the situation of the lyric with the situation of the grief, only an attempt to give a personal and beautiful gift to another person who was in grief. The lyric, in the reading, this time began to be lyrical. Then the actor asked the student to stand behind the grieving man, to rub his shoulders and neck muscles as he spoke the words of the gift-lyric. The lyric, in this reading, was pure beauty. The student had found his own voice in an imaginative but nevertheless real situation. He could at that point face an audience and speak the lyric with conviction and sensitivity, perhaps even with that wondrous quality—the unfeigned spontaneity of a man who has relaxed enough to accept himself, to speak with his own voice, to trust it in the speaking, and to trust those who will hear it or read it.

I share this notion at some length with you today because I believe it has a real lever force on helping us, you and me, understand the whole business of making a speech, of making a piece of writing, of making a college, of making a world, and of making a life. Somehow, each of us must find his or her voice, be willing to hear the sound of that voice in spoken and written word and to live with the sincerity of those words at any and at every moment. Your voice, my voice, will be shared with many others, will be formed by the interplay with many others—but my voice can never be a copy of any other if it is to be real; neither can it be a synthesis of many other voices. The real joy and the real terror—the mystery of life—is to speak to life as it exists at any given moment; to open oneself to life speaking to us at any given moment, speaking to us always through persons and events and physical phenomena. The man or woman who is afraid to respond will never find a voice. The young student at Stanford who found his voice by giving a gift-lyric to a grieving man opened himself, even in physical movement, to the aches of that grieving man. A genuine response is never hollow words or the cold and hollow detachment of an intellectual scheme. A genuine response is the caring and care-full honesty, the genuine spontaneous feeling of one man for another, or of one man for all the other men who live or will live.

E. M. Forster speaks to this point in a powerful essay entitled "What I Believe," written in England in 1939. He says:

> One must be fond of people and trust them if one is not to make a mess of life, and it is therefore essential that they should not let one down. *They often do.* The moral of which is that I must, myself, be as reliable as possible, and this I try to be. But reliability is not a matter of contract—that is the main difference between the world of personal relationships and the world of business relationships. It is a matter for the heart, which signs no documents. In other words, reliability is impossible unless there is a natural warmth. Most men possess this warmth, though they often have bad luck and get chilled. Most of them, even when they are politicians, want to keep faith. And one can, at all events, show one's own little light here, one's own poor little trembling flame, with the knowledge that it is not the only light that is shining in the darkness, and not the only one which the darkness does not comprehend. Personal relations are despised today. They are regarded as bourgeois luxuries, as products of a time of fair weather which is now past, and we are urged to get rid of them, and to dedicate ourselves to some movement or cause instead. I hate the idea of causes, and if I had to choose between betraying my country and betraying my friend, I hope I should have the guts to betray my country. Such a choice may scandalize the modern reader, and he may stretch out his patriotic hand to the telephone [like the McCarthyites and the John Birchers] at once and ring up the police. It would not have shocked Dante, though. Dante places Brutus and Cassius in the lowest circle of Hell because they had chosen to betray their friend Julius Caesar rather than their country Rome. Probably one will not be asked to make such an agonizing choice. Still, there lies at the back of every creed something terrible and hard for which the worshipper may one day be required

to suffer, and there is even a terror and a hardness in this creed of personal relationships, urbane and mild though it sounds. Love and loyalty to an individual can run counter to the claims of the State. When they do—down with the State, say I, which means that the State would down me.

This brings me along to Democracy, "even Love, the Beloved Republic, which feeds upon Freedom and lives." Democracy is not a Beloved Republic really, and never will be. But it is less hateful than other contemporary forms of government, and to that extent it deserves our support. It does start from the assumption that the individual is important, and all types are needed to make a civilization. It does not divide its citizens into the bossers and the bossed—as an efficiency-regime tends to do. The people I admire most are those who are sensitive and want to create something or discover something, and do not see life in terms of power, and such people get more of a chance under a democracy than elsewhere. They found religions, great or small, or they produce literature and art, or they do disinterested scientific research, or they may be what is called "ordinary people," who are creative in their private lives, bring up their children decently, for instance, or help their neighbours. All these people need to express themselves; they cannot do so unless society allows them liberty to do so, and the society which allows them most liberty is a democracy.

Democracy has another merit. It allows criticism, and if there is not public criticism there are bound to be hushed-up scandals. That is why I believe in the Press, despite all its lies and vulgarity, and why I believe in Parliament. Parliament is often sneered at because it is a Talking Shop. I believe in it because it is a talking shop. I believe in the Private Member who makes himself a nuisance. He gets snubbed and is told that he is cranky or ill-informed, but he does expose abuses which would otherwise never have been mentioned. Occasionally, too, a well-meaning public official starts losing his head in the cause of efficiency, and thinks himself God Almighty. Such officials are particularly frequent in the Home Office. Well, there will be questions about them in Parliament sooner or later, and then they will have to mind their steps. Whether Parliament is either a representative body or an efficient one is questionable, but I value it because it criticises and talks, and because its chatter gets widely reported.

So Two Cheers for Democracy: one because it admits variety and two because it permits criticism. Two cheers are quite enough: there is no occasion to give three.

This is one of the longest quotes I have ever given in a public speech. I think I have a right to quote such a long passage, one which dedicates itself to the subject of voice, because I think I can speak Forster's words with my own voice, because they are words I recognize from the depths of my own being and recognize in another human being and speak not his words but my own through his.

Mr. Forster spoke with a real voice in 1939 in a world just awakening to the reality of Fascist Spain and Nazi Germany. His democracy and our own were being forced to listen and even to respond to voices which were bringing about the destruction of six million Jews, voices that were silencing public criticism, voices that were dividing "citizens into bossers and the bossed—as an efficiency-regime tends to do." And the democratic world found its voice almost too late, paid and made all civilization pay in the anguish and tragedy of World War II for the voice it could not or would not find until terror was in sight. And when it found its voice it responded in the voice of atom bombs, a voice no free man ever wants to use again. The democratic world is always in such danger, because freedom of speech implies the freedom not to speak, the freedom of refusing to take a stand to respond to life as one sees it oneself, rather than as one feels one is expected to see it. I would maintain that there is no voice of democracy, only the *voices* of democracy, as many voices as there are real persons, responsible decision-makers in a society. A chaotic world indeed if there be as many voices as there are persons—chaotic and dynamic and productive in the hold-together tension force of atoms in a molecule, acting and reacting, speaking and responding in a force of dynamic unity.

If there is a person in a family who is discouraged from finding his voice, the family is in trouble. If there is a person in a college who is discouraged from finding his voice, the college is in trouble. If there is a person in the church who is discouraged from finding his voice, the church is in trouble. If there is a person in a nation who is discouraged from finding his voice, that nation is in trouble. If there is a person in the world who is discouraged from finding his voice, the world is in trouble. They are bound to be in trouble, because the family, the college, the church, the nation, the world exist for persons and inasmuch as they deny personal dignity to any person they have literally sold their *birthrights*—their right to existence.

It takes a family of deep courage and faith to create a climate that encourages the youngest member to find and develop his voice. It takes a college community, a church, a nation, and a world of deepening courage and faith to create that climate too. This faith is faith in the potential of personhood, and the courage, I believe, is in direct ratio to the depth of that faith in the potential of persons. If I really believe in an Aryan supremacy of any kind in the Hitler sense, I try to create a world, be it a small world or the great world which will be a society of the bosses and the bossed, the tellers and the told, the supervisors and the subjects, the dispensers of rules and regulations. If I really believe in democracy, if I really believe in *human rights* (of which civil rights are an important but limited part), I try to create a world, be it a college classroom, a college campus, a parish, a city, or the world-at-large, which will be a society of co-searchers, a society of co-learners, a society of caring conversationalists who speak with a real voice and listen to other real voices in the conviction that only so can we see and know and do a little more together. And in the seeing and the knowing of the little more together, we may be able to do again a little more together.

We often hear speeches (or give them), we often write articles (or read them) on the subject of freedom and responsibility. I would like to suggest that we consider freedom the necessary climate in which *authority* and *responsibility* operate. By authority I mean the authority of an author who signs his work, who speaks with his voice, his conviction, his very soul. Such an authority, such an authorship, produces something worth saying only if the author is responding, is responsible, to reality in more than a superficial way. We have all been part of small talk, the words that fill up silence but do not touch us. Small talk is probably unimportant if it encompasses only picayune things, though it can destroy a man or woman if he lets his life be dominated by this kind of mock heroic. But small talk is a kind of prostitution if it speaks to great issues, if it speaks hollow words in response—or lack of response—to real persons living real lives of joy and anguish because the speaker cannot or will not respond to those real persons.

Economists and educators, politicians and theologians, faculty members and students can talk *about* issues or they can speak *to* issues; speak to those issues through the persons involved in the issues, by allowing themselves to become involved to some degree in the situations that make the issues. And if you do not become involved in some way—in a real way—in the situations that make the issues, then and only then do I think you or I are guilty of the prostitution of great issues by small talk, by superficial gossip, by uninformed and irresponsible comments. I speak to you today with the only voice I can find, my voice calling out to yours for response —real response—so that I can respond to you, so that the climate of freedom in the college community (which only our voices, yours and mine, can create) will produce authority and responsibility in each one of us. Not authority in me and re- sponsibility in you, but the shared commitment of co-learners, co-searchers, who believe that I will find my voice as you find yours, that you will find yours as I find mine, and that the growing force of those voices of democracy will have their own hold-together tension like atoms in a molecule—acting and reacting, speaking and responding in a force of unity.

I will have the courage to find my own voice, inasmuch as I trust you to let me find it; and you, the youngest student in the audience, will have the courage to find your own voice, inasmuch as I your president, these your faculty, and—equally important—that student sitting next to you convey to *you* the trust of letting you find your own voice.

This world, even the fraction composed of free thinkers, is afraid of this kind of honesty; afraid to speak it, afraid to ex- pect it, afraid to develop it. For such honesty produces the chaos which is inseparable from freedom. It takes a trustful and a courageous man to live with chaos at any given mo- ment and try to bring structure out of the chaos and responsi- bility out of the chaos. This is indeed a frightening kind of honesty.

If persons, some called administrators, some called faculty, some called students, but all co-learners, co-searchers—con- templative human beings who have not a ghost of a show of knowing what life is really all about in one lifetime—can engage in such an action-conversation at Webster College during this year, our voices will have something to say to a world and will elicit an important response. But it is important to each of us and to the world that the action-conversation in which we will be involved not fall into small talk but touch and be touched by urban St. Louis and rural Mississippi, by Vietnam and Vatican II. We must not be content to carry the sandwich-board signs of the latest developments in St. Louis and Mississippi, in Vietnam or in Vatican II, the sandwich-board signs which record the latest pronouncements of the voices of authority. If we really believe that the Church means we are the People of God, and that the Spirit speaks in each of the members, we will find our voices in the college and in the world. Then and only then can we become the authors of our own actions responding to a real world, and coming to a real moral integrity, which can exist only in the human person who is not looking for a crutch or any easy way out. If we open our persons to such a real world, if we open our persons to other real persons we will find our voices and they will be heard, but more wondrously (most wondrously of all) we will begin to find ourselves.

If men or nations were compelled to believe that the answers they propose today are final and irrevocable, I submit that both men and nations would be rendered immobile.

Commencement Address
Skidmore College
June 4, 1967

Since I am a good decade past that magic age of thirty, I ought to approach this platform knowing that there is no chance of communication between thee and me. Let me assure you that at least I shall not deal out to you any of the old platitudes about entering out into the world, about entering into life. To say such things to a generation that has lived much in this world would be ludicrous indeed.

You have lived your entire lives in a permissive culture which is at the same time part of a world which controls your actions and your very lives. Young men you know and love are being drafted to fight in a war about which many of you have ambivalent if not negative feelings. At such moments when you and I seem powerless in the powerful grasp of a mass society, we struggle to try to understand our responsibility for the very power of the society of which we are a part.

Raised and educated in a permissive society which has granted you the favors of affluence, you are baffled as you realize that that society often becomes rigid and rejects your attempts to modify it in any way.

It seems to me that students all over this nation are asking really radical questions about the nature of authority. Is the authority of a nation, of a church, of a corporation, ever absolute? Is there any formula for ethical or moral behavior that holds in every case in every time? Is man really responsible *to* authority and/or is he responsible *for* authority? Are you as individuals, or is some superstructure above or around you, the real author of your actions?

A couple of years ago I had an intriguing conversation with a magnificent older gentleman in the St. Louis area. We have been friends for a long time. Despite the fact that he is ultra-right politically, and though he recognizes me as a liberal Democrat, he continues to support me and the emerging nation we call Webster College. On this particular day, I was in his office to work with him in raising a substantial amount of money for the college. He immediately confronted me about the early news of students burning draft cards. "You see," said he, "it's all this permissive education that you believe in that brings about this kind of nonsense." I answered: "Maybe that's so, my friend, but let me ask you some questions." I then asked him what he would have done had he been a citizen of Nazi Germany in the early thirties. I told him that I hoped with every fiber of my being that I would have committed operational treason, that I would have harbored Jews. I am not sure I would have had the insight or the guts to do so, but I hope that I would have. He agreed that he could see some credibility for this position. "If this is so," I said, "do we not at least have to admit the *possibility* that operational treason at some point at some time might be heroic virtue?" He answered quickly: "Yes, but not in the United States." We then went on to discuss the whole business of moral responsibility in your generation at this moment in time.

My position now is essentially the position I took with him that morning in his office. It is not yet a popular position with my own generation or with many of my colleagues charged with responsible authority. My position is quite simple. Unless we in authority in the universities, in the churches, in the corporations, and in the state and federal governments have the simplicity, the humility, and the courage to face the possibility that there is always at least a very small probability that authority should be put in functional question by responsible deviant behavior, then you indeed should charge us with credibility gaps that may widen into chasms. Only if we admit this .000000 . . .001 probability that operational treason may be heroic virtue, is there any viability in our insisting that the weight of authority in most cases may hold .999999999 . . . force and effectiveness. If absolute obedience to absolute authority is always virtue, then Eichmann was the greatest of the saints.

You and your children and your children's children's children's children will come to moral responsibility in your personal lives and in the societies you will continue to make only if you begin to understand and to incorporate what it means to be a finite man in finite time. The norm of behavior, the laws under which we live today, are the attempt of other finite men in finite time to come to terms with their fallibility, to make the best approximations they could manage given the limitations of their insights at the time of their decision-making. If you and I believe that we indeed live in an evolutionary world, then we see that world and all its artifacts as continuing approximations toward approximated goals. I am becoming more and more convinced that man is *defined* in his realization of his finiteness, of his fallibility, and of his responsibility in acting within his limitations. If men or nations were compelled to believe that the answers they propose today are final and irrevocable, I submit that both men and nations would be rendered immobile.

I have the courage to act because I so profoundly believe that you and your generation—breathing down my back, eager to seize the reins from my hands—will modify the contribution I and my generation will make, both because and in spite of our successes and our failures. Each man's vision of his personal and social responsibilities at this moment is some paradoxical resolution of the expanding and limiting power of his experience. When one has dealt with the problems of college administration or of world government over a period of many years, one indeed has a range of experience that contributes to vision. But roads traveled over and over again have an obvious facility for turning into ruts. This is why we are so dependent on the corrective and often disruptive power of your own inexperience, which will propose to us the alternative behavior which our very experience blocks us from seeing.

A fine scientist friend of mine giving a commencement address a couple of years ago made the statement that all committees ought to be made up only of those who would be responsible in carrying out the decisions of the committees. His second criterion for committee makeup was that all such committees ought to include the very best professionals in a field and always some very bright amateurs. The old may very often be the very best professionals, but only the young, the uninitiated, can play the role of the very bright amateurs who ask the brash and sometimes rash questions opening up new vistas and new possibilities for man and men.

All of us are aware of the mounting tensions in domestic and foreign affairs which have become not the exception but the very day-to-day realities of our lives. The emerging minorities at home and the emerging nations abroad have begun to discover the power of authority. They have begun to author their own actions and to bear the consequences of making personal decisions. No longer is man content to be the passive recipient of the "charity" of more favored men or of more favored nations. Your generation either blasphemes God or sees it as a blasphemy *to* God if religion becomes the guardian of the *status quo*. What kind of father would bless the selfishness of one brother who would use his status to hold down his younger brother?

Perhaps only a few grandparents today remember with any firsthand knowledge the company town of less than a century ago—company towns in which one man controlled the destiny and the day-to-day life of all other men and their families in that town. Much like the plantation system of master and slave, the day-to-day life in many ways depended on the benevolence of the master. But that day is gone. It seems to me that man is struggling between two radically different notions of society. One is the tribal culture, the imperial system, the absolute monarchy, the monastic cloister: all had their internal consistency in earlier ages. In such systems the only concept of obedience was obedience *to* authority, and this kind of obedience was the only path to moral responsibility. In such systems, the subject was morally responsible if he obeyed, and the authority was morally responsible if he gave orders. But there is a second notion of society which demands that we begin to realize the terrible responsibility of decision-making. We do not, I believe, necessarily join the marchers in the latest protest whatever it may be. When we begin to realize the awesome responsibility of decision-making, we may, however, risk ourselves and our reputations to act responsibly according to our conscience. Every rational system, every constitutional government, every institutional form has been forged out of the new and growing experience of men. The very notion of subsidiary democracy, of representative government, is dependent on forming responsible deciders of their own destiny.

John J. Chapman, writing at the turn of the century, stated that "perhaps all truths whether moral or economic, must be worked out in real life before they are discovered by the student." He gave as an illustration the activity of William Lloyd Garrison, a man of action, which preceded by several years that of Emerson, who was his prophet. Chapman insists that both of them were parts of one revolution.

Your generation, it seems to me, is irrevocably cast in the role of action in an open world emerging from the isolations of tribal cultures. Like it or not, *you* must forge out the new systems which can cope with the passion for integration and internationalism and religious ecumenism which are surging everywhere in our world. The tribal code and mores of self-contained and isolated little worlds are no longer viable because the tribes are no longer impregnable. Men and societies must learn to integrate themselves, somehow to come to terms with the conflicting views of other men and other worlds around them. Tribal cultures were supportive of clannish arrogance, whether it was in a school, an ethnic community, or in a nation. The world society where instant communication is becoming more and more possible, and even inevitable, cannot fall back on these kinds of external crutch moralities. To the man indoctrinated in the formula kind of moral code, the divergent moral behavior of the young seems always to be licentious. Indeed, you the young would politely laugh at me were I to suggest that all of your divergent behavior was moral heroism. But you and I both know that the hippie community and the bastions of black power are not categorically the powers of darkness while the orthodox *status quo* represents the powers of light.

If peace on earth is more than a fiction of the imagination or, worse, a Machiavellian rationalization for warmongering, then your actions, reached through the anguish of responsible decision-making, must forge new concepts of world government for the generations to come. If the family of man, even in this nation, is not to be a figment of the imagination or a sentimental rationalization of white "charity," then your generation must continue to invent those individual actions which will save us from ourselves.

Small men in great nations will do everything in their power to preserve the *status quo*. They may indeed be successful in their own lifetime and preserve for themselves and their clans the supremacy of their station. But great men and great women in great and in emerging nations will invest themselves in the force of the future. They will become responsible *for* authority, and through their authorship they will continue to invent a world in which their children's children will indeed rise up and call them blessed. Perhaps it is merciful that none of us knows which of you will choose the first or the last investment. If your education has permitted you—indeed, compelled you—to assume the responsibility for making decisions and living with their consequences, many of you, I believe, will invest in the force of the future.

II   *The Communicators*

If education is a communication of life power, if it is the communication of physical life, intellectual life and moral life and affective life . . . if it is indeed a communication of life and a transference of grace, then it is the most exciting enterprise that man has ever been about. It may indeed be what man is.

—*February 15, 1967*

*If the students on our campuses are disturbed by the present
kind of compromises that we have to live with; if at the same
time they are grateful for the creative compromise that we have
managed in our time; then they will be the makers of tomorrow.*

University of Missouri
February 15, 1967

Many of us today talk about not only formal education but
about the whole educating society—the whole body politic, the
whole family of God—in which we are all teachers, professors, learners, students, sometimes learning from one to the
other and sometimes learning in reciprocal fashion, learning
because others pose to us questions for which we do not have
integrated answers; learning because we allow ourselves to
pose those questions to our students and allow those students
to pose them to us. The body of fact, the body of knowledge,
and the body of insight a man has acquired is the most
powerful lever he will ever have on searching and researching
what may lie beyond. But paradoxically we know at the same
time that this body of knowledge, this body of expertise, this
proven way, is sometimes the very limiting factor that closes
in our probe even as it opens it up. The naïveté, that precious

naïveté of those young students who ask us questions, may be the liberating force that saves us from ourselves.

This does not mean turning education over to students or throwing away the concept of authority. But perhaps it means looking at a new kind of authority, *the right of authorship*. The man who authors an action must be the man who is responsible for that action. The man who authors an action must be the man who lives with the consequences of his action; or, in my opinion, he is acting irresponsibly. He is not authoring in a responsible way.

When I talk about education, I talk not so much about curriculum, or courses, or faculties, or stratifications of knowledge as about the communication of life and grace, because I am convinced that this is what education is all about. If education is a communication of life power, if it is the communication of physical life, intellectual life, and moral life, and effective life (and the students today are becoming increasingly concerned about affective life), if it is indeed a communication of life and a transference of grace, then it is the most exciting and stimulating and challenging and frightening enterprise that man has ever been about. It may indeed be what man is.

What do you do with your own children? You communicate to them *life*. You communicate to them life—biologically and symbolically and beautifully in an act of love. You make them in an act of love. But you make them every day, and you make them every week, and you make them every year in communicating to them . . . what? Standards? Knowledge? Or communicating to them life?

Many people can no longer pick up a phone and call their mother and father. I still can, by some grace, as they still live at the other end of a telephone, on a farm up in Illinois, 52¾ years married, and are still able to communicate with me: not to direct me, not to own, not to possess, not to judge, but to love and to support. They are communicating life to an individual, communicating their life which will be in me, and *must* be in me long after they are not at the other end of the phone. This life will dwell in me, not possessive of me, but never to be taken from me—this life which was given to me, not just when I lived in their home, but which is always there because it is a staying force, a loving force, a supporting force.

If, indeed, we are beginning in our time to see the human family in this context, if we are, indeed, beginning to live in an age of internationalism, integration, and ecumenism, then perhaps—perhaps—we have begun to discover the way to give a man power, to communicate to him life and trust, not judgment, not suspicion, not failure. The ability to say to a man "What do you do?," not "What can't you do?" The ability to say to a man, a boy, a child, and an old man who is never old "What would you like to do?" How many divergent ways can we find for a man to become *who he is*?

The greatest parents are the parents who give their children the freedom to be who they are and who somehow or other communicate to those children the grace, the life power to support one another in their divergence. If this is what God's family is meant to be, then it seems to many of us that we have got to relax, we have got to smile, we have got to allow for divergent ways we cannot understand. Because each of us is a finite man, in a finite time, with finite information, with finite experience, and the only way we can be powerful is to be humble and to know that we have a limited insight for which we are responsible. But we must also know that there is no way we can demand of every other man that he walk in our shoes or in our paths.

How does man incorporate life into himself? How does man become who he is? How does a student at the University of

Missouri at Kansas City or at Webster College or at the little elementary school, or in a Headstart program begin to become who he is, or how does he go on being this? It seems to me that he incorporates into himself not what the Chancellor tells him, not what the Headstart teacher tells him; he incorporates into himself that which he perceives. He incorporates some piece of it, he permutes it, in the mathematician's sense, he puts it together in some sense of integrity for himself.

We have long been baffled by the fact that the FBI cannot find two thumbprints that are alike. Perhaps the notion of a thumbprint is the most beautiful notion of permutation in mathematics you can ever get. If we can take a space *that* big, and if we can take lines and permute them in some way; and if we can combine them and discover that no two thumbprints, no matter how hard we try, will ever be the same (at least we've not *found* two that are the same!), then how can we find two men who are the same? Is my thumbprint an integral whole? Is your thumbprint an integral whole? Is anyone's thumbprint an integral whole? But how can they be integral if they are not the same? How can we have responsibilities if they are not all the same? They are integral because they make sense, because they make one whole, because they are not falling apart and diffusing. Every individual, whether he studies mathematics or science or life or ultimate reality, is, in my opinion, attempting to make by acceptance and rejection the choices which will make him whole. He selects many of these things deliberately; he selects some of them permissively; some of them partially; some of them perhaps almost unconsciously. And life lies all around us like the seed in the ground. Sometimes we do not even know that the seed is there because it hasn't had the right sunshine. I want to call it latent life, that seed in the ground.

James Joyce, the Irish writer, in his notebooks for *A Portrait of the Artist as a Young Man* talks about life, and learning, and loving, as an Epiphany, as a manifestation, and he says we don't learn $1 + 1 + 1 + 1 +$ as on a linear line, but rather that we learn in flashes. We have all kinds of discrete pieces of information, all kinds of insight, all kinds of talks we have heard and books we have read. We might call those experiences A, B, C, D, E, F, G, H, I, J, K. For everybody there is a different *Gestalt* pattern. Then I am asked a new question, or I look at one waterfall, or I see one demonstration, or I am terrified at the inhumanity done to one person. And in comes a new letter X or omega or "belaquick," in comes some new piece of information, and it does not just get added to A, B, C, D, E, F, G, H, I, J, K, plus. Rather it goes in and it *transfuses* and it *transforms* and *reintegrates* and gives a new integrity to the shape of all of those things which have been there before. Joyce calls this an Epiphany. He calls those the moments of manifestation, the moments of life when each man reintegrates —does not pick from but reintegrates—all of the learnings, all of the life, all of the grace, all of the authorities he has possessed before. It is this concept that I have kept for at least the last ten years of my life in trying to make some kind of sense out of life when it is terrifying and wondrous, contemplative and frustrating. But always life with a growing edge, always life with a deepening focus.

If we are structuring and integrating our knowings and our perceptions, we are deepening our power to go on perceiving and knowing, but we are also deepening our power to get hurt, because we are making ourselves more and more sensitive human beings. We are making ourselves more and more conscious of how terribly finite we are.

At a talk in Chicago about two years ago, I used an image that I have not used recently. I told the audience there that I remember waking up in the middle of the night several years ago and realizing that I was .000000 . . .001 of the human race. And the dots are what are important, because nobody knows how many dots, nobody knows how many zeros, nobody knows when it is over. Is 1967 the beginning of mankind or the middle of mankind? Have we yet gone through the bend in the exponential in the evolution of nature? Has the curve yet done this? Are we still on that beginning base line? Is the bend in the curve yet to happen? Is the big push going to happen in 2555? Who are going to be your children's children, in something like 2650? Is the world still going to be around? What are men going to know in those days? You and I have not the faintest notion, but we do know that we live a life in which there is continuity. We do believe that life is a continuum, and whoever is alive in 2065—if the world has a shape in 2065—will indeed be your children's children; and the evolutionary generational process will have gone on. The only sustaining thing that man can have is life and grace—not rules, not codes, not static norms. The life you communicate to your children biologically, and to the human family environmentally and lovingly and supportingly, is the life that nobody can take away from us, the life that is communicated in us, that is incorporated in us, that is made our own because it dwells in us.

In my estimation, the curriculum projects in the academic disciplines have been fascinating in the last few years, not because they deal with mathematics or science or anthropology or any specific disciplines. Despite all the labels they have been given (the "discovery process," the "inducted method"), the real emphasis, it seems to me, has been on pattern-making. It has been an attempt to get a student to perceive a sense of pattern. If the student sees a sense of pattern existing in history or in his present environment, he can begin to improvise patterns that man has not yet seen. Where is the pat-

tern that can solve the racial hazards of our country? Where is
the pattern that can solve disarmament? Where is the pattern
that can take away the necessities of universal conscription
and requiring men to kill? If we do not listen to our students
on the campuses of these universities, if we do not listen to
them when they ask hard questions, even if their answers
seem to us supercilious and gross; if we do not listen to them
when they ask those questions, we are not communicating
life to them. We are not communicating to the generations
after us the kind of power that will someday give to man a
clue to disarmament and universal charity in the world.

When one says this, one is accused of being a dreamer, an
optimist, a nonrealist, a nonpragmatist. I want to say just the
opposite; I want to say that the age of science, the world of
science has opened up to us the pragmatic door to humanism,
the pragmatic door to real spiritual growth and power. I believe this to be so because science has respected the finitude
of man; science sees itself no longer as the open door to per-
fectability. Science has perfected and given to us at a radical
level the very notion of incremental gain, the very notion of
success of approximations; and those notions are among the
most powerful notions that man has ever had. I would argue
that they are among the most spiritual, the most religious notions man has ever had. Because they say to man, *you are
responsible; you must do what you can do;* but also *you can
not do it all.* You have got to be able to hand it over to the
body politic, to the family of God; you have got to be able to
share it with all other men, and you have got to know that
your children's children's children's children's children are
going to outdistance you—precisely because you gave the
power that you did not have; precisely because you asked
some questions that gave to them the feedback data to drive
them to have more understanding.

But more understanding is that new disturbing factor that throws what was the structure into chaos again, so that it can be reintegrated at yet a deeper level and a deeper meaning. The patterns of history and the patterns of society in an environment provoke the prophets of tomorrow. Not the Utopian prophets but the pragmatic prophets, the prophets who will make love, the prophets who will make the world, the prophets who will make the human family. The mother who is a successful mother is the mother who is most terrified of her responsibility but most willing to meet it.

The most important anecdote of my own personal life took place in two settings. One was in the Executive Office building of the White House on the day after the second Cuban affair. Dr. Jerome B. Wiesner, who was Mr. Kennedy's science advisor, came into a meeting that I was attending and said "Jacqueline, walk down the corridor with me. You and I have often talked about humility and courage," he continued, "I still don't know how to define them, but I want you to know I'm sure I watched them yesterday." He had watched Jack Kennedy look nuclear warfare in the face to know it was there, to know it was possible, to know there existed some moment in time that was better than any other moment in time, some degree of force that was better than other degrees of force, some juxtaposition of that moment and that degree of force that was better than any other juxtaposition, to know that he was the President of the United States and that he had to make a decision and he didn't have a hell of a chance to hit it, but that not to make a decision was to make the worst possible decision. Wiesner said: "I can't define humility and courage, but I know I watched them yesterday."

Thirteen months later, I was in a hotel room in New York City alone when I heard that first terrible announcement that the President of the United States had been shot. I went through all those hours unable to cry. I walked the streets of New York and went to St. Patrick's and tried to pray, came back and glutted myself with the television playbacks, trying to make some sense out of the world. Late into the night, some station replayed the Rocking Chair Conference in the Oval Room of the White House. Earlier in the interview, one of the network men asked: "Mr. President, were your advisers wrong in the Bay of Pigs?"

"I don't know," Kennedy said, "I was the President of the United States, and I obviously took bad advice."

About ten minutes later, Sander Van Oker, who was his friend, played the role a friend always plays, the compassionate, loving, supportive role: "Mr. President, were your advisers right in the Second Cuban Affair?"

Kennedy, with that beautiful sense of humor that one wishes all Presidents shared, said: "I don't know, I was the President of the United States, and I obviously took good advice."

And with that, all of the grief and all of the terror welled up and I wept in my hotel room alone, and I remember beating the pillow and saying aloud, over and over to myself, "My God, that's the kind of human being I want to be." Counterpointed against the knowledge that the President was dead were Wiesner's thoughts thirteen months earlier: a moment in time and a degree of force and some juxtaposition of that moment and that degree of force, and he was the President of the United States and he had to make a decision and he didn't have a hell of a chance to hit it. Somehow, that says for me in a graphic image what life is all about, what education is all about.

Education is the conviction that we are finite men in finite time, confronting decisions for which we will be responsible, for which there will be sanctions external, or inherent in our responsibility to other persons; but knowing that we are falli-

ble and that we can be wrong—knowing also that to be totally inactive and unable to move is to be finally irresponsible.
I believe this should be the fountainhead and the base, at the
root of all of our educational systems.

If indeed we create a system in which a student is afraid to
make a stand, in which the sanctions are too early and too
hard for making a stand, we will create a "stable" 1984 bureaucracy of the managers and the managed, of the authorities
and the subjects. But we will not have the kind of responsible
society that democracy must have if it is to avoid chaos, and
worse than that, the rigidity of 1984. I would argue that responsible skepticism is the most important cognitive, spiritual,
affective, moral holding a man can have.

Let me say clearly that I do not believe I would burn my
draft card (it's a ridiculous kind of situation, because I am a
woman and at the time I was thirty-eight), but hypothetically
I do not think I would burn my draft card. But having said
that, I would say to you that the individual must always have
the right and the responsibility and the *necessity* at some
point to take into account an authority that does not seem to
be the "proper" authority. Only if we admit this to students
can we say to them that there is a strong probability that authority in major concerns ought to be heavily weighted. I believe that unless we will say to them that any human being
could be wrong; the Chancellor could be wrong; I could be
wrong, can we ask for them . . . *from* them the kind of responsible action that comes, I believe, from responsible skepticism, not dilettantism, iconoclasm . . . not that at all, but
man living with the integrity of his conscience.

Modern science has given us the notion of "feedback"
mechanisms. It has given us the notion of the self-correcting
principle. Modern life has also given us the notion of passive
resistance initiated by Gandhi and interpreted by the Negro

movement in the U.S. The integration movement, I believe, will prove to lead to great grace, life, power principles for your children's children. The so-called racial integration will be only one of the consequences, one of the beginning consequences, of what those active in the integration movement will have taught us. Because at their best—not in their mistakes, not in their gross attempts, but at their best—I think they are teaching us what responsible decision-making is all about. They are teaching us that man can author any action if he is willing to live with the consequences of the action; that law, whether it be mathematical law or civil law, or a law of economics, implies and necessitates first of all a respect for law, a respect for law as being the sustaining notion of keeping society together. We must have a respect for law, a responsibility for law, a responsibility for communicating respect for law coupled with a responsible resistance to law at any given time. How else does law get made and modified? How else do we get evidence from which we generalize the laws that must come? How else is a man to live with the paradox of respect for law, responsibility for law—and resistance to law? How is a man to live with this paradox of structure and integrity—and not anarchy? It seems to me he can live with it only if he *pre-accepts* the consequences of his decisions.

Whether or not one is a Christian, whatever one believes about a divine being, it seems to me if you read the gospel message of the Christ, its "sociological" message, you find that the heart of the gospel message lies in two principles: look at these people how they love one another; and secondly, what the Christ called "detachment." What is detachment in our time? Fundamental detachment in our time is nonrespect for the pecking order. Fundamental detachment has a lot to do with the man who is willing to lose his life in order to find it;

the man who is willing to accept the consequences of a decision even when he does not know what those consequences
may be; the man who goes to jail—if he indeed believes that
in helping to *make* the law, on rare occasions he must *resist*
the law, but not resist the *sanction* of the law, because that is
what law, not anarchism, is all about. The "detached" people
in history, in my estimation, were these responsible heretics
and skeptics. Responsible, not irresponsible, not Utopian, the
men who were willing to live with the consequences of their
decisions and did not hate the people who placed the sanctions on them. I would argue that society always needs critics.
We have the beginning of a great world and of a great nation, but the nation has not faced the problem and potential
of an international society.

What of students and responsible skepticism? If the students on our campuses are disturbed with the present kind of
compromises that we have to live with; if at the same time
they are grateful for the creative compromise that we have
managed in our time; then they will be the makers of tomorrow. You and I must be convinced within the radical pit of
our being that unless the generations are more powerful than
we are, we will have been failures because we will not have
given them life and power to go on. Only if we are convinced
of this can we be real educators. Only if we are really convinced of how little we know can we possibly have the detachment rooted in the great faith which will allow us to live
with the unknown.

I deeply believe in God—more deeply than I ever have in
the past. I do not know who he is. I think it would be blas-
phemous for me to define who He is and to lock Him up, to
say He is this and no more. Because at the radical pit of *my*
faith is a conviction that I, in some way I cannot define, will
contemplate Him forever . . . forever, and I will never ex-

haust Him. Can we not give to our students on the natural and supernatural level this kind of faith, this kind of power? Who is the person who can live with the unknown? Who is the person who can live with what he cannot yet handle? He is the person who is loved and supported. He is the person who has given life and grace and power. Not the person who is watched and who is going to be sanctioned for having tried. If we have the courage, it seems to me, to communicate these kinds of notions, to open ourselves up to this kind of detachment, there will be generational gaps only in knowledge; not in power.

I visited an apartment in Greenwich Village some time ago. There was a group of interesting people there: a fine Georgian gentleman, an elder statesman of education, Peace Corps officials and Peace Corps volunteers, and an intense young man who led part of the revolution at Berkeley. He is a "trip-taker" with long curly hair and bearded face and blue jeans. I was able to watch the confrontation of the elder statesman and the young Berkeley "student." It was beautiful to watch; it was beautiful to be part of! The young man began to talk about a contemporary of mine whom I respect a great deal, a "middle-aged activist" rooted in the style of the Socratic seminar, Harris Wofford. In a burst of emotion our blue-jeaned friend said (let me use his words or it does not make any sense otherwise) "Damn that Harris! No matter what you say to him, he tries to incorporate it into that Socratic dialogue . . . no matter what you say to him about communication that is at the affective level, at the gut level and not at the rational level . . . he tries to incorporate it into that rational mechanism." He went on and on with this, making beautiful lyrical sense and nonsense, and then in a burst in the end, he said "But he is tormenting and he is honest, because in his attempt to make radical sense out of all of this, he is willing to live on the edge and to blow his system, man, by being logical and by filtering but not rejecting what he doesn't yet know how to incorporate. Man, you can't dismiss that kind of honesty!"

If we are willing to live on the edge responsibly, if we are willing to say to each other—and if we are willing to say to Russians and Chinese and Germans and Hindustani and Africans and Berkeleyites, and trip-takers—if we are willing to say to them that we live on the edge; that we will at least *incorporate* their questions when we cannot incorporate their answers or their nonanswers; then I think we will become the educating society, the contemplating society, the family of man. I believe, at the depths of my being, that we live at the dawn of a new spiritual renaissance because we are becoming the wondrous, contemplative men of tomorrow. I believe also that there is no age limit for us who are willing to live on the edge—to live there responsibly; to know that we cannot do it all; but to know that we are infinitesimally powerful, each one of us, and that the life we communicate to one another tonight, and tomorrow and the next year and next generation will somehow be incorporated in some way if it is to exist, in our children's lives.

If the students can see us as honest and clearheaded, as persons who cannot solve everything that is here to solve today; if we open up to them our own terrors and our own troublements; then, and only then, do I think we can communicate with them.

National Conference of Association of
College Admissions Counselors
Washington, D.C.
October 6, 1966

I should like to share with you one of my favorite ancedotes about my friend and predecessor, and in many ways my spiritual mentor, Sister Francetta.

In her work for the Women's Job Corps, Sister has often been used as a troubleshooter for the very trouble-shot Office of Economic Opportunity. She was sent, among other places, to St. Petersburg, where somebody had mistakenly placed the Women's Job Corps in a hotel across the street from a hotel housing retired citizens. (All of us who are in college work have some notion of what it is to have that kind of birdwatcher across from a conventional dormitory!) At any rate, the Corps was in great trouble, and a Chicago *Tribune* writer, who I hope meant well, was writing editorials which were scalding the Office of Economic Opportunity. Sister Francetta had been sent down to try to calm the troubled waters. After she got back to Washington, Mr. Shriver came down to her office one day and said, "Sister Francetta, brief me quickly. I've got to go to The Hill to testify about St. Petersburg." Sister began to brief him, but he decided they'd do a better job if they both went to The Hill, so they rode up the long drive to the Capitol and came into a hearing in a congressman's office. Shriver wasn't doing very well, and he turned to Sister: "Hey, Sister Francetta, tell them that story you told me on the way over here."

Sister, who has her own kind of love for a stage and the simplicity to admit it, staged a performance. She told how she was walking into the Women's Job Corps one night about nine o'clock with some other women. As she was walking in, she noticed an old codger bent down looking in the window. Sister went up to him, tapped him on the shoulder, and said, "Good evening, sir, how are you?"

He leaped up, very embarrassed, and said with a deep Irish brogue, "There are bad girls in there, wicked women."

"Well, sir, what makes you think that?"

"Why, everybody says so."

"Now you know better than to form your decisions on rumor and hearsay. Do you have any evidence?"

"I do," he declared firmly.

"What's your evidence?" demanded Sister.

"I was walking down the street the other night. I was minding my own business, and two of those brazen hussies came up along the street and they accosted me."

"They accosted you! Why, what did they do?"

"They came up to me and with *no provocation* they said, 'Good evening, sir. How are you?'"

Sister looked at him. "Why, sir, I just came up to you and I just said, 'Good evening, sir, how are you?' and I'm a Roman Catholic Sister!"

He got into the middle of his next sentence before he heard the words. Then he burst out, "Glory be to God, what did you say?"

"I said to you, I'm a Roman Catholic Sister."

"Saints preserve us, and *you* look like *that!* What have we come to!"

Sister said, "Yes, and I look like *this* because I believe so much in those girls up there, and whether I'm right or wrong, I think I've got a better chance to work in their behalf by looking like this."

Then he said, bewildered, "You mean you think I'm wrong?"

And she said, "Yes, I do, but I can tell you're a very bright man and that you're going to get better evidence on your own."

The old man thought about it a while, then looked at her and said, "You think I'm wrong. . . . All right, *All right*, I'm going home, and I'm going to say the rosary. I'm going to say the rosary twice. Once in case I'm wrong. But the other time for *you*."

The story means a great deal to me. I think that it has a great relevance to an area that I want to open to all of us to think about. I have roughly entitled my remarks "Moral Sensibility or Sensitivity." It seems to me very proper and very right to discuss this kind of subject with a gathering of persons belonging to your association: persons who have given themselves to a profession of counseling; persons who are freer than most, I hope, to be *person*-oriented, to be *student*-oriented rather than institution-oriented; persons who are free to think of institutions as existing *for* students, and not to think of students as existing merely to fill slots in institutions. I think this is terribly important. If you are freer than most, freer by situation even than *I* can be as a college president (I

have to work harder at it), then it seems to me that you must
be among the first to look at the student climate as it is developing in our colleges and universities today, and you must not
be too easily deceived by externals. Please God, you will not
be the first to determine morality by beards or nonbeards, by
sandals or shoes, or by other of themselves inconsequential
aspects! Certainly you will not fall into the trap of some public school administrators who think of themselves as liberal
and yet throw people out of schools because their hair is too
long, under the pretext that there is some reliable correlation
between length of male hair and immoral actions. I asked one
of them not long ago why he didn't criticize the evil actions
rather than the bad hair if he could see a correlation so well;
why did he not keep his sanctions clearly dependent on the
thing he was criticizing?

We hear a good deal today, and I hope we read a good
deal today, about what's been called The Movement. The best
estimates of the number of students who are in The Movement is somewhere in the neighborhood of five per cent. But
some very insightful people are estimating that up to fifty per
cent of the students in our colleges and universities not only
on the West Coast but across the country are now sympathetic and compassionate about the five per cent who directly
see themselves as involved in The Movement. I would much
rather call it The Movement than the New Left because I believe that the New Left is an inaccurate term. I think we
would make a very bad mistake were we simplistically to
identify The Movement as a kind of Communist-inspired
activity.

In many senses The Movement is as anti-Communist as
anything could be. If we really believe that communism is an
ideology, a closed ideology; if we really believe that communism is dependent upon indoctrination, then The Move-

ment is philosophically anti-Communist because The Movement, for all its bad and good attempts, is really looking for a
world of pluralism. It is really seeking, in its blundering way,
for a world of honesty.

William Robert Miller wrote an article called "Christianity's
New Morality" in *The New Republic*. In that article he says:
"The radicals are prepared to accept as morally valid a whole
range of formerly proscribed behavior, but what makes theirs
a 'new morality' rather than 'no morality' is that they are looking for basic criteria." They are looking for basic criteria by
which to guide conduct in the light of some ultimate purpose
rather than leaving moral choice to the mercy of whim and
caprice. He goes on to say there is a recognition that decisions
cannot be made in the abstract. Decisions arise in a context of
circumstances, and this situational context not only modifies
the application of law, but also defines the issues that are involved. One thing the churches have learned from the struggle for racial equality is that in some situations civil disobedi-
ence is preferable to the loveless use of law. I want to suggest
that what we call the passive resistance movement in the
United States may, if we continue to see its potential, be the
savior of democracy.

The cutting edge is always small. Its solutions may be
wrong, and therefore it is desirable that it should be small.
Harvey Cox, in his very illuminating book *The Secular City,*
traces for us all a fundamental thesis that I think we must
look to and that has great relevance to what we are thinking
about. Cox makes no attempt to give us a blueprint for the
future. He quite honestly, I think, in the book and in his writings about the book, defines his role as the role of prophecy,
prophecy which is always gray rather than blinding white or
darkened black. Cox traces for us his thesis of the evolution of
man from what he calls the tribe to what he calls the town to

what he coins as *technopolis.* He says that man in tribal culture was dominated by the world of myth, myth in its best sense. Man in the town was dominated (as was our medieval society, which was characteristic of the town) by ontology, by the definition of the abstract truth. Technopolis, Cox says, is being dominated by secularization. Cox makes a very great distinction between secularization, which he sees as a process, and secularism, which he sees as a new closed ideology. Within this distinction he champions secularization, the process by which man demythologizes his tribal culture. Now, in my own view, man in such a world becomes the contemplative man, the deeply spiritual man who realizes he is confronting infinite reality and infinite truth, but recognizes the fallibility of his own race, and the finitude of his time; and therefore knows that he will for all his finite time and finite space be *fallible* man making successive approximations toward a limit that none of us can comprehend.

Within his book Cox suggests that the characteristics of modern man are "pragmatism" and "profanity." By pragmatism he means the tactical approach of biting off what one thinks may be manageable, or working on what one thinks may be manageable, and of trying to avoid the pitfall of believing that what is manageable is all there is. He suggests that the main proponent of pragmatic man in our time was John Fitzgerald Kennedy, who, though he believed in a hereafter theologically, knew that man must work in the now. Man must work with the limit of his own ability in the now. Cox sets up as his proponent of profanity Camus. He defines profanity in its purest sense, not in its popular sense, as a removal from the sanctuary. That which is profane is opposed to that which is sacred and set apart. He suggests that Albert Camus, like every atheist, was a particular kind of atheist who was rebelling against a particular God-concept; and that

Camus was rebelling against the God-concept of Western man which had shown God all too often as stripping man of individual responsibility and decision-making. Whether or not medieval Christianity really made that stand is not, I think, the important issue. The important issue is whether or not modern man *sees* that as Christianity's stand. In a day when we perhaps are to preoccupied with "image-making," we must at least be aware that what a man hears is not always what we meant to say. If the majority of modern men have heard that Western Christianity has limited the responsibility and scope of decision-making, then we either have to clear the view or yield the stage to new kinds of insights.

Man *is* fallible. Man *is* finite. Consider any world leader who has before him the awful responsibility of facing decisions when he cannot know that he is infallibly right. To make no decision is to make the worst decision of all. If that is true for national leaders in time of world crisis, then it must be true for you and for me and for every student in our high schools and our colleges today. Decision-making must be the essential human act.

It seems to me that students are looking in their blundering way for some kind of integrated behavior. They used to talk of "phonies" during the days of J. D. Salinger. Today they talk of "finks." Finks are worse than phonies. I am sure that sometimes in my life I have been a phony and I am sure all of my life, because I am a tactician, I am in danger of being a fink. I think students are interested in structural choices. I think they are trying to find a way to make choices that fit, that make structure because they fit into an integrity that they can get hold of. In that sense the most important thing we can share with them, the most important component of modern education, I would submit, is responsible skepticism. Responsible skepticism in my view is the only possible antidote to

1984 and *Brave New World.* The bureaucracy is here to stay. There is no way to go back to the sanctuary or to Walden Pond. We must find a way within the bureaucracy, within the secular city, to find a new spirituality, to find a new kind of compassion, to find a new way that respects the human person. One of the thrilling insights of Cox's *Secular City* is his suggestion that the anonymity of the modern city may provide the new way for man to be personal. Man, because he is anonymous, because he is nakedly alone in many situations, has the press and the opportunity to be morally responsible.

I suggested to my students, in a lecture to a class for which I was a guest professor, that we might think of the world as being split into the persons whom we would call purists, tacticians, and opportunists. I define an opportunist as the person who makes his decision by what is expedient, and I want to rule him out of my value system. I want to be called every time anyone sees me acting as an opportunist! I would call the tactician the pragmatic man, in whatever part of life he happens to find himself, who meets the decision in finite time and tries to handle it operationally, responsibly bearing the consequences of his decision. I would define the purist as the honest man who is a visionary, who tries to describe a Utopian world, but who decides that he will remain free of the operational responsibility precisely so that he may fulfill the role of prophecy more clearly. I want to take a stand strongly, with my students and with myself, championing both the purist and the tactician. By nature, by circumstance, and I think by desire, I will spend most of my life in the role of a tactician. But having taken that position I need, the purist to keep me honest.

I was thrilled when I learned that Secretary McNamara, then Secretary of Defense, in his troubled appearance at Amherst, stopped at the moment some of the Amherst faculty and the students walked out of his commencement address, stopped and waited for them to leave, and then said "It is always difficult to bear that, but I vote all the more strongly for a United States in which it is possible." It meant much to me, for I need to believe in Robert McNamara in these troubled days. And I need to know that Robert McNamara is capable of voting for responsible skepticism even when it hurts him most. The purist, however, needs to respect the tactician because the purist, if he is not to become arrogant, if he is not to become smug, must realize that he has decided not to play the responsible game of action. He must not let himself fall into the smug, childish position that we all play when we are Monday-morning quarterbacks. Having chosen not to decide what plays to call on Saturday or Sunday afternoon, we must not smugly stand on Monday morning and say if we had only been coaching we would have done it all the right way. The purist needs respect for the tactician to keep him honest.

I am in admiration of some of the administration of Stanford University at this moment. Stanford University has as its president of the student association David Harris, who is the acknowledged leader of the movement of the New Left in the United States—bearded, sandals, all the rest. Try to imagine what it would be to be a responsible fund-raiser for Stanford University! Try to imagine what it would be to be dependent on funds from the alumni, the Board of Trustees, and from the business interests if you were at Stanford University! I met the Dean of Student's Joel Smith, at Stanford recently. He spoke with real feeling and concern about David Harris and said with simplicity that he strongly believes that Harris may be a Christ-figure. Hard to take. Hard to handle. Even to deal with in one's mind. I asked him what position the Vice-President for Development, who is an old friend of

mine, was taking. I was almost afraid to ask. And Joel Smith
answered "Lyle Nelson is my strongest supporter."

I want to meet young Harris someday, and I shall. But I
want to find out whether young Harris, who I think is an
honest purist, has it yet in his being to recognize the heroism
of a Lyle Nelson, the tactician. I am suggesting to you that it
is a two-way street, and that unless we look at the heroism of
both we will never get anything like the honesty of comple-
mentarity.

Authority and responsibility must be co-terminus. Man cannot take any responsibility for something if he is not the
author of his actions. But inasmuch as man is the author of his
actions, he has got to bear the responsibility of those actions.
He cannot give away the consequences of those actions. The
passive resistance movement has been speaking for divergent
behavior with a respect and an acceptance, a preacceptance
of the sanctions that go with it. In this sense Martin Luther
King may be asking us all to confront the most important les-
sons modern man has yet to learn. If we can accept the responsibilities for our decisions by preaccepting the world in
which we live, then and only then can we know what radical
detachment means. If the Spirit of the Gospel says anything,
the Spirit of the Gospel affirms the radical detachment that
allows a man to escape the pecking order, that allows a man
to take a position even if by taking that position he might lose
his job. When students talk about "finks" they are talking
about our becoming captives of the system in which we shove
off the responsibility of decision-making by saying "But that's
what I have to do!" I simply cannot do that. If the students
can see us as honest and clearheaded, as persons who cannot
solve everything that is here to solve today; if we will open up
to them our own terrors and our own troublements; then, and
only then, do I think we can communicate with them.

I met Daniel Berrigan, the Jesuit poet-priest-social actionist, in an airport in Washington two weeks ago and spent an hour of pure joy with him. Berrigan said to me "Talk to me about Francetta," and I did a little. Then he said "You know, Sargent Shriver says over the length and breadth of this country that Francetta is the greatest single input of hope and joy that has ever walked into the United States government." Berrigan, who has known severe criticism, could appreciate the kind of letters she gets from all kinds of well-meaning people who think that she's an old lady in her second childhood who is escaping reality. I told him that I knew she preaccepted the sanctions of that passive resistance out of her commitment to a fallible position and a finite position. The young people in this country, the ones in my college, the ones in the Peace Corps, would "dig" her. Not because of what she wears. That is incidental, except it has an integrity to the wholeness of what she is doing. They would "dig" her because they would say "She's honest. She's willing to say that she doesn't know what it's all about. She's willing to keep on working."

There is a big businessman in St. Louis, a right-wing conservative, who has become one of my dearest friends. He is the chairman of the board of a big corporation. The very first time I ever went to visit him, I was talking about foreign languages in the school, trying to raise some money for the project in elementary education. It was seven years ago. And five minutes into the conversation he said to me "Are you pink, Sister?" I didn't know how to answer, so I kept on talking about foreign language in the schools. He wanted to talk about American history. After a while he took me on a tour of his plant, took me into his board room, and had me listen to a record of an American Firstist named Paul Harvey. We went through all the glories of America, and thank God I didn't have a flag to raise! In the middle of the record Harvey declared, "We, seven per cent of the world's population, control fifty per cent of the wealth." (And you are supposed to wave your flag!) When it was over I must admit I capitalized on the image of naïveté that I could then capitalize on (that's when you're a tactician), and I said to my friend "For we, seven per cent of the world's population, to continue to control fifty per cent of the wealth, would this have to be done at the price of slavery of the other ninety-three per cent?"

He replied, "That's a very provocative question."

We left, and the banker who was with me said, "Sister Jacqueline, you've lost your mind. Nobody in town talked to him that way. You threw $5,000 out the window."

"Perhaps I did, and if I did, I did," I answered. "I need it badly, but I couldn't let that lovely man think I agreed with that. But I bet I didn't. I bet he respects the courage of convictions. He is a rugged individualist. We'll see." Two days later he called me at a quarter of eight in the morning. (He *is* a rugged individualist.) And he said "Sister Jacqueline, my Board just voted you that $5,000, and I want to tell you how much I enjoyed the conversation. I hope to know you a lot better." Then I would hear dribbles of conversation from civic gatherings in which he would say "You know that young Sister Jacqueline over at Webster College came over, and she crossed me, and I gave her $5,000!"

Over the years we have become real friends.

This same businessman was helping me raise money for a building fund. He gave me from his company the first $50,000 and he's helped me get to other people. I walked in one day to get some help on money-raising and he glowered. "I'm mad at the St. Louis nuns." I knew well why he was mad at the St. Louis nuns. We had been in a civil rights march. He was getting sterner and sterner.

"Now look, my friend," I said. "You and I have a lot of respect for one another. Is that right?"

"Yes."

"The reason that we have a lot of respect for one another is that we each have the courage of our convictions. Is that right?"

"Yes."

And then, again being a tactician but an honest one because I mean this, I put my hand on his arm and said: "But the proof that you and I have a lot of respect for one another is that we trust one another enough to *expose* those convictions to one another, and I'll bet, my friend, there aren't ten people in the city of St. Louis who want your money who trust you that much."

And he had big tears in his eyes when he said: "That's right."

We sat down and talked for twenty minutes about civil rights. I asked him if he'd ever known a Negro who was his peer. You know, he knows about *seven* men who are his "peers," who go to the exclusive clubs and all the rest. But he'd never thought this way. I submit that's the reason we are friends today, and he could hear me tell this story knowing I wasn't telling it in derision, because we trust each other enough to be honest. He would know that I am one of the few people who don't think he's a "fink" because I would know where he's been—in the limitations of his tribe (and there are *socioeconomic* tribes, just as there are *academic* tribes and *church* tribes and all the rest!). In his tribe there is a very closed system, and most of us who are the finks, who are the phonies, want to *use* the people in this socioeconomic tribe. We want to use them for everything we can get out of them, and so we never tell them the truth. We don't respect them enough. We don't trust them enough to tell the truth. If our students are telling each other the truth and sharing the quest for truth and couldn't care less about telling *us* the truth, then it's because they think we aren't capable of hearing the truth as they see it. They don't think that we're capable of the radical detachment even while we preach morality up and down the line.

Sister Francetta told the president of Notre Dame, Father Hesburgh, that every time she meets a businessman who goes on a tirade about morality in the Job Corps, she makes a one-to-three guess that he's a graduate of Notre Dame. The only reason I can tell this is that it says something about the greatness of Father Hesburgh and of our relation to him because you can say that to him. Because Sister Francetta and I also know that every time I meet the suburban women who are John Birch moralists we also know they are possibly graduates of Webster College. And this says to me "What did we do?" and "What didn't we do?" and "What have we done to make moral judgment, rather than compassion, the keystone of the religious world?"

The young people in their blundering attempts are more spiritual than I ever thought of being at nineteen. They are more concerned in their blundering gray way with the dignity of man—even in their wild attempts to solve it through LSD—than I ever thought of being out of my provincial background at nineteen. But if we close the doors to them, if we suggest that to be skeptical is to be a traitor, a traitor to the United States, a traitor to our academic institutions, a traitor to our churches, I think we make them take their movement away from us.

I've said to students and I say to you, at the risk of losing my White House clearance—and I will continue to make this statement out of loyalty to the United States, out of loyalty to the Roman Catholic Church: unless there is somebody like a Teilhard who had the courage to put away his writings when they were proscribed, and to send them to somebody to keep until the people woke up—unless there is that kind of passive-resistance courage—neither the United States nor the Church will remain responsible or vital.

It is this vision, I think, that we must share with students. John Henry Newman and many others have reminded us that there are no blacks and whites, but only varying shades of gray. If we can live with the gray; if we can live with pluralism; if we can live with divergent opinions; if we can give people the respect of their own integrity, and not say that my integrity must be everybody else's integrity; then, and only then, I think, is the passion for integration truly evident. The integration of pluralism of our times is shown poignantly in the civil rights disturbances in March; is shown, I think, perhaps even more graphically for the ages to come in our struggle for international peace and unity; is shown brilliantly in the beginning insights that we are getting into ecumenism where man stands back and says: "I am fallible man searching, privileged to search with every other man, for the truth I cannot yet hold and will never be able to hold." Only in this realization do we become a humanistic culture, children of God, brothers of each other, loving each other because none of us thinks he is infallible.

I cannot afford to question the institution that is my college without the insights of my students.

American Council on Education
Washington, D.C.
October 8, 1965

I am grateful that the title "Higher Education and the Moral Revolution" refers to a moral revolution rather than a revolution in morality. I am convinced that the seemingly chaotic state of things dramatized, but not contained by, the campuses of Berkeley and St. John's may say much to those of us with eyes to see and ears to hear and hearts to care. You and I—young or older academics—have emerged from a culture which often identified morality with moral codes and expected behavior patterns. Each church group, each academic community had its own group-determined grading system for group-determined answers to group-determined exam questions. Morality was largely an expository codification much like a driver's manual in a given state. We had to learn the rules—and how to break them with impunity—in Michigan and Missouri, in New Mexico and New York. We took verbal tests on the manuals in ethics classes and action tests on the manuals under supervision. We violated specific tenets in personal situations, sometimes with guilt, sometimes with rationalization, sometimes with conviction. But it seldom occurred to us to question the manuals for their inclusions or exclusions. We learned to live within the system or systems. Sometimes we compromised the system here and there, and no one bothered too much if our compromise did not alter the basic system too much. Sometimes we compromised ourselves by accommodating to the system and its expectancy behavior demands. But most of us lived within fairly closed societies, and the expectancy behavior demands of any one closed society are, I submit, fairly predictable. Mine were the demands of a parochial Roman Catholic environment. Yours may have been the demands of a parochial Bible Belt fundamentalism, of a Jewish ghettoism, or of a smug atheistic intellectualism. Whatever our closed systems, they provided for us a degree of comforting support by that closed system. Objective moral codes had to be learned and basically adhered to, but they need not—indeed, perhaps must not—have to be personally made.

I submit that the moral revolution we are witnessing on our campuses today is indeed calling the codes into question and rightly so. In my own subsystem, students are not only "violating" some of the carefully calibrated norms of morality behavior with guilt and/or rationalization, but they are calling into question the validity of many of the tenets themselves. The present soul-struggle of my Church today in re-examining its stand on birth control is motivated much more, I believe, by the responsible skepticism of the Church's own members than by the pressure-concern of the Rockefeller Foundation concerning overpopulation. I am sure that some of the fundamentalist groups have long been meeting the same responsible skepticism over drinking and dancing and cards. I am sure, too, both from the rush of articles in popular magazines and from common sense, that more sophisticated religious groups and sophisticated student personnel officers are meeting responsible skepticism over any fixed and given propriety in sex relations and in marriage laws that attempt to cover all possible situations with a single prescription or proscription.

At this point I am obviously vulnerable to the charge that much of the skepticism, on both the theoretical and pragmatic levels, may be totally or largely irresponsible, that human beings always have and always will use rationalization to cover their own license and weakness. I accept the charge even before it is made. At the same time, I suggest that our challenge at this moment in time is to accept the skepticism, to encourage it, to nourish it, even to share in it. It is difficult to encourage or demand responsibility for an area of action in which we have forbidden or discouraged or ignored concern and questioning. Inasmuch as we, as academics, as religious people, as concerned humanists, admit the need for responsible skepticism in every human area and, therefore, in every moral area, we will begin to give our junior colleagues, whom we call students, the responsibility of freedom. Only if a man is allowed to frame his own question can he be really responsible for his own answer. Only if your students are *encouraged* to frame ever more relevant and profound questions can they be really responsible for relevant and profound answers. And the freedom which will allow them to frame relevant questions will always mean that they will frame many irrelevant questions as well.

I have said that the moral revolution on our campuses today is, indeed, calling the code-prescriptions into question and rightly so. The most encouraging phenomenon of the questioning is its preoccupation with the "sins" of *omission* rather than the "sins" of *commission* of the codes. The Puritan-Jansenist codes had much to say about sex and sobriety but precious little to say about the human rights of minorities and the force of passive resistance. The Puritan-Jansenist codes had much to say about responsible behavior but precious little to say about responsible skepticism, about the compromise society has made at any given time on any given social issue. The comparative closure in which we lived even in the pluralistic society that is America made it comparatively easy, I believe, for the codes of each of the closed systems to endure.

Today, however, you and I in middle age, and our students in the blessed and productive naïveté of youth, live in what I have been calling the ecumenical world of search. Transportation and communication have potentially, at least, destroyed the ghettos of nationalism. The open and instant press has potentially, at least, destroyed the ghettos of religious thought and reopened the channels of religious thinking or contemplation. The system of higher education beginning to open itself to all socioeconomic, national, religious, racial groups will experience with growing intensity the stimulation and disorder of this ecumenical searching. The social and philosophical and religious and moral systems will be subject to the personal pressure and cross-pressure of persons interacting in an open society. Students in such an open society within a college or university are not likely to allow the college or university to remain segregated from the real issues of Vietnam and Vatican II, of Watts and India. For the world of open communications reaches into the ivory tower, the fraternity house, and the sanctuary, and asks the ivory tower, the fraternity house, and the sanctuary to respond to the real world.

Teilhard de Chardin, the Jesuit paleontologist who died in 1955, wrote in an essay in 1920:

I maintain that it is possible, by following this road, to find substantial reasons for belief in Progress.

The world of human thought today presents a very remarkable spectacle, if we choose to take note of it. Joined in an inexplicable unifying movement men who are utterly opposed in education and in faith find themselves brought together, intermingled, in their common passion for a double truth: namely, that there exists a physical Unity of beings, and that they themselves are living and active parts of it. It is as though a new and formidable mountain chain had arisen in the landscape of the soul, causing ancient categories to be reshuffled and uniting higgledy-piggledy on every slope the friends and enemies of yesterday: on one side the inflexible and sterile vision of a Universe composed of unalterable, juxtaposed parts, and on the other side the ardor, the faith, the contagion of a living truth emerging from all action and exercise of will. Here we have a group of men joined simply by the weight of the past and their resolve to defend it: there a gathering of neophytes confident of their truth and strong in their mutual understanding, which they feel to be final and complete.

It is "the ardor, the faith, the contagion of a living truth emerging from all action and exercise of will" that can produce, I believe, the social, moral, intellectual, evolutionary breakthrough that modern man needs and must have. Only persons who are responsible skeptics and responsible decision-makers can effect such a breakthrough. You and I, the middle-aged academics, are part of one culture involved in producing another; part of a culture of two world wars trying to produce world peace; part of a racist, segregated society trying to produce integration; part of a ruggedly individualistic capitalism trying to produce personal responsibility and social concern; part of a moralistic religious society trying to allow the morality of empathy and compassion. Perhaps the only honest and productive force we can produce is to allow ourselves to join with our students in the ecumenical world of search to produce the new worlds of our own academic institutions and of our society at large. I cannot afford to question the institution that is my college without the insights of my students. Neither can I afford to question my world at large without their blessed naïveté! I do not believe it is our world—or our values, or our morals—to be preserved *for* them; but our world, our values, our morals always to be found—*with* them. I can encourage them, and myself, to examine and re-examine every tenet of the present codes lest our skepticism be irresponsible and superficial. Neither they nor I can lightly disregard the tenets of the codes. However, only if I merit their trust by the honesty of my own scrutiny in its rigor and its freedom can we become co-searchers and co-makers of the society which one day you and I must leave to them—our students—that they may continue the search and the making with their children yet not conceived.

To be segregated is always to be deprived.

Magazine Industry Seminar
Harvard Business School
July 2, 1964

I think perhaps the most deadly thing that any one of us has to face is an in-group climate in which we keep talking to ourselves and convincing ourselves of that with which we have already been indoctrinated. It is for this reason that I wish to talk to you today about the open society, the values of an open society, the critical value of the open society in our world. I am here to maintain that "to be segregated is always to be deprived."

I believe that in the field of race this is just as true for the "overprivileged" suburbs as it is for the inner cities. But it is also true of socioeconomic classes, true of the professions, true certainly of religion and philosophy, of national and ethnic groups.

There is a very exciting book called *The Christian Commitment* by Karl Rahner, the great German Jesuit theologian who was very controversial at Vatican II. Rahner was one of the theologians who was held off by the Roman Curia and embraced by John XXIII. In *The Christian Commitment*, Karl Rahner says that we are living in what he calls a Christian diaspora. He goes back to the Old Testament image and talks about the Jewish Diaspora, the condition of the Jews who went out from Jerusalem into pagan lands where they were no longer a Jewish community but were Jews of the dispersion. He transfers this image into the Western culture of our time.

At one time we were the Christian West. In this sense Christianity was nominally at least co-extensive with the nations themselves. And so we had Christian education, Christian culture, Christian esthetics, Christian art, and Christian social institutions. This is no longer true, he says, because we, the Christians, are in the minority; we are in the minority everywhere. And so we must be Christians of the diaspora, reduced or exalted to our individual worth. We are now Christians *in* education, Christians *in* art, Christians *in* social welfare. Because, as Rahner says, these are functions of the whole people; they must never be subcultures. It is this kind of thesis that fascinates me at this time.

It is much more important that any member of a subculture be a person involved in a greater culture than that he operate from the—I think—debilitating position of the subculture itself.

What I am trying to say is that ghettoism or provincialism is always debilitating. It is more debilitating to the group that is practicing the segregation or the provincialism or the parochialism than it is to the great culture. But it also deprives the great culture, because here is an enriching and a hybrid kind of contribution of which the great culture is being deprived. And so I have practically lost my head at times by saying that it seems to me, from our point of view, absolutely the worst thing that could happen to us to achieve the old-time ideal of every Catholic child in a Catholic school.

A couple of years ago I said to my Cardinal, for whom I have great respect: "Suppose that the United States were to accept the position of so many pressure groups and were to agree to support private religious schools either directly through the schools or through the parents. Then suppose we were told we would be given *equal but separate* rights." If such an offer were made, I hope we would be bright enough to say "Don't do that to us. You have already done that historically to the American Negro. And we know from his experience that unless you are a full and a participating member of the whole society you are not a full influence in that society. You are not a completely interactive member of that society."

And so it seems to me, from what I would call apostolic reasons, not from legal reasons, that this would be the most deadly thing that could happen to the education of Catholics. I am talking now not about Catholic education but about the education of Catholics, which I consider much more important.

It is the education of persons which is important. It is the person who must make decisions; it is the person who must act with free will. It is the person who must choose from alternatives. We live in a highly sophisticated society [a society where in the words of Newman, there are no blacks and whites. There are only varying shades of gray,]. We simply cannot wait for someone to push a button and tell us what to do in our philosophic or in our moral standards. We must learn to handle alternatives and to do the very best we can with our limited intelligence.

This, all of it, I think, has profound implications for the whole field of communications. It is here that I think I do share in your world, because I am convinced that the field of communications is as proper to formal education as it is to the world of periodicals, and as proper to the world of periodicals as it is to formal education. I think all of us are convinced today that formal education can be only an opening wedge, an opening wedge to the learning process which I hope each of us will be indulging in until we run to our graves. Then, if there be an eternity, and I believe there will be, I hope that learning process is going to go on forever and ever and ever because I cannot think what else contemplation could mean.

If this is true, if we are going to indulge in the learning process forever, or at least if we are going to indulge in it until we run to our graves, then all of us who are involved in the field of communications, in interpersonal relationships of the mind, must consider what kind of learning theory we believe in.

I think that there are two polar learning theories and many ramifications between. One I shall choose to call indoctrination; the other I shall choose to call insight. And I would suggest that the radical groups that we have heard so much about are always guilty of indoctrination. Be they the Communist left or the John Birch right, it is because they are guilty of indoctrination that they are dangerous. Because they subject people to monolithic thinking, to platitudes, to a conviction that one can make simplistic kinds of judgments, they somehow rob us of that aching, full-of-wonder reality that life is tough but wonderful; that one has to operate within limits and make the best judgments one can make with his finite mind at any given moment; that there is no such thing as being absolutely sure.

Many of us, from our ghettos, have been subjected to and guilty of this kind of indoctrination. We have been guilty of it in our schools; we have been guilty of it in our religious groups; we have been guilty of it in our economic groups. We always indoctrinate out of what we see as a kind of security orientation. We are saying "Let us give our children the security of a foundation. Let us not *worry* them."

I would answer to this kind of judgment that the only security a late-twentieth-century American or a late-twentieth-century world citizen can have is what I shall call *the security to be insecure.* This is the fundamental security we must give to our persons in our society. We do live in an open-ended society. It is open-ended geographically. It is open-ended ideologically. It is open-ended scientifically. It is open-ended philosophically. The counterpressures are everywhere, and I think they are vitalizing counterpressures.

The physicist who lives in his lab knows that he may not solve the thing he is trying to solve, even in his lifetime. But he doesn't stop trying to solve it. He is excited to the chase by the fact that he has a finite mind which is pushing back reality by what he calls successive approximation, pushing it back and back and back. Operating in that glorious unknown, he has to work, at least in the field of his endeavor in his laboratory, with the security to be insecure. He knows that he may have to change his pace; that he must watch phenomena; that he has to have a radical kind of intellectual humility if he is going to be honest—the intellectual humility to confront facts, to confront reality, to confront processes, and to change his mind on what was his hunch. I would suggest that we need this personal posture just as desperately in our social situations, in our philosophical situations.

I would like to say that we, in my particular subgroup, have done a terrible disservice to a man like Thomas Aquinas. Because, if Thomas Aquinas was great, and I think he was, his greatness lay in the fact that he was able to ask the most profound questions of his time. But, if Thomas Aquinas were living now, his greatness would lie in exactly the same ability to ask profound questions of the present data. Thomas Aquinas did not have the data we have. There have been generations of evolution, intellectual evolution, since his time. And we make the terrible mistake, I think, of canonizing a man, in secular as well as in religious thinking, for what he *found* rather than for the *process* of his finding. We worship the static image instead of the dynamic process. In doing this I think we make the ironic mistake of freezing what our great creative thinkers managed to do. A creative thinker is always a man who is ahead of his time. If a man is a creative thinker in 1800, the thrust of his mind projects decades ahead. If the same man were living in 1900, he would be thrusting forward from 1900, because he would be the same kind of man in his time that he was a century earlier. This I think is true of our statesmen, true of our religious thinkers, true of our philosophic thinkers, certainly true of science and technology and business and industry.

Those of you who represent one of the burgeoning industries of our time know this. I will not mention names for fear of being accused of vested interest, but I am sure that there is one publishing group, thought of by some people as a monster in the publishing world, that perhaps more than any other has evolved on the principle of research and development. This enterprise has really gone off on wings; it keeps trying one thing after another; and in this sense it has been able to grow and grow. There are probably other groups for whom this has been true, too.

One of the most thrilling experiences one can have in the St. Louis area is to go out to the Monsanto Company's research and development campus on Lindbergh Road, and go through that research and development complex. One day the director of the research labs was taking me through. We walked into a

lovely concert hall and there was a fellow playing a harpsichord. When I asked if he were giving the concert that night,
the lab director replied; "Oh no, Sister, he runs one of our
research teams. He's liable to play that harpsichord all day."
Then he chuckled. "But he might have a great idea tonight."
I told this to a group of suburban-school-system teachers in
University City in St. Louis and I said: "Can you imagine
what the local school board would say?"

All of this says to me we must make up our mind whether
we want the security of the 4½ per cent savings account,
which admittedly we sometimes need, or whether we want to
play the market. If you are successful as a gambler, you are
courageous; if you are unsuccessful as a gambler, you are
foolhardy. But one has to be able to face either option. One
has to have the kind of security to be insecure if one wants to
gamble for the great end. Some of us are saying we must look
at our institutions this way.

Any institution which has been around a long time will not
be able to remain vital if it holds onto its vested interests. I
am convinced that what educators call the "Hawthorne effect"
is perhaps the most precious thing we have in the principle of
self-renewal. It is the very spillover, the very vital life of experimentation, that makes things good. As soon as we lose
that quality of experimentation, the vitality and the life go
right out of the process. What we must do somehow is to do
what the great corporations have done. We must *build in* a
Hawthorne effect by building the whole spirit of experimentation and innovation into every one of our industries.

We may be accused of considering only a small percentage
of people in such an approach. David McClelland pointed out
the consistent pattern through history of a small elite sphere of
influence in any society and posed the problem of reconciling
personal achievement and social responsibility in society. In

McClelland's terms, what are we talking about? Are we talking about a little group up here △ that is going to manipulate society because you make them highly inventive? I would say that we must talk about more than those people. Maybe we can bring the active group down ▲ , but I am even more worried about these people △ , the more passive members of our society. I am worried about the masculine and feminine old maids who are terrified by our society, the people who are most susceptible to indoctrination because they want something safe and secure. They want an ostrich hole that can protect them from the tensions of life. I would submit that the more passive members of our society are in great need of realizing that we live in an innovative society and must come to terms with that innovative society. If they can watch people innovate in school as well as in the rest of the learning world, perhaps they can more easily come to terms with this. One of the mathematicians whom I respect a good deal was presented with this problem: "Of course you can go to a group of third-graders and get some children doing quadratic equations and linear functions and matrix algebra and not just learning terms, but inventing mathematics. But can you get every child in that classroom to do it?" He answered first of all by saying: "Did you ever get every child in a classroom to add properly?" But then he went on to something much more important. He admitted that they do not all invent at the same rate, and perhaps there will be some who never really invent at all, but at least they will live in a mathematics classroom in which they recognize that the essential habit of mathematics is invention. They will not be duped into thinking that mathematics is some kind of a computational security where people falsely believe that this is one world where you can have right and wrong answers.

The McClelland evidence that economic growth shows a

close functional relationship with first-grade readers is certainly interesting. If this is true, and I suspect it is, then we must be awfully careful about what we do in the early years of learning. If we believe that we can *indoctrinate* students with the American dream or with a religious point of view; if we believe we can indoctrinate them, and then expect them to live in a highly tense world in which their very security is dependent upon their spirit of inquiry—the spirit with which they can inquire in tension—then, I think, we take the final safeguard away from them. They will be utterly frustrated by the experience of the open society, which is always evolutionary.

Another exciting book, written many years ago but suppressed for a long time by my own church and now republished, is *The Phenomenon of Man,* in which Teilhard de the level of thinking man, the stage of evolution becomes self-conscious evolution. Teilhard, a paleontologist, was a respected evolutionary theorist. He suggests that when we reach the level of thinking man, the stage of evolution becomes self-reflective and therefore self-directing; that man can now, to a large extent, qualify the direction of evolution. He suggests that just as the scientist observes that we have had many misfires for every breakthrough in materialistic evolution, we are now witnessing many misfires in what he thinks is the great breakthrough to social man.

That we are now trying to arrive at some idea of social man in the continuing process of evolution intrigues me. Now I am sure if there were representatives of the John Birch Society or their counterparts in our midst, I would immediately be called a deep shade of pink. To clarify my position, let me pick up again what McClelland said about our being involved with our two great needs: developing an achieving, ambitious, forward-thrust society and at the same time developing a society conscious of its fellow man. This is a paradox, a seeming contradiction. It may be the greatest paradox-challenge that lies before us. Most of us have anything from a third to a half a life to go on trying to conquer the paradox, to achieve the resolution. We must somehow try to develop a new kind of man, a new kind of woman, who realizes it is virtuous to be ambitious, that each of us has only one life to spend. I like to say to young women: If I went into a dress shop and I had fifty dollars and the choice of wearing something other than this, I am sure that I would find five or six things I'd like to buy. Then I would be forced to decide on which one I would spend my money. I like to look at my life this way. I have one life to spend. The decision of where to spend it is the most important decision I shall ever make. If I believed in reincarnation—and I would almost like to believe in it at this point—I would like to try architecture on one go-around; I would like to try physics on one go-around. It is fascinating to think of the number of things you can invest your life in! But you make a commitment, and you work within those limits, and you try to squeeze out of that commitment—not by the talent in the napkin, but by foolhardy or courageous investment—everything you can for your contribution to this great corporation which is the world community. If we can ever begin to communicate this to students, then I think we begin to get a new kind of ambition, a new kind of achieving society which sees its achievement as building the world community.

A friend of mine reminded me that it is more important to start a revolution than to write a satire. And perhaps we have had very many too many people writing satires, empty satires. The satires, I think, belong to the nineteenth-century romantic poets who wrote ivory-tower satires that offered no resolutions, no first hunches, no first approximations, but con-

demned all of society around them. The poet took on the role
of the high priest without the commitment of the priest. This,
I think, would be terribly dangerous in our society. On the
other hand, the responsible involvement of one who is willing
to go in and make some of the hunches and to live with the
hunches and to say he made mistakes if his hunches turn out
to be wrong, and to remake some others, could reshape and
remake the American society.

We have today the most ecumenical kind of spirit, not only
theologically but also personally. A new kind of ecumenical
spirit is, I think, deserting the old debate technique which
ruined us all. This new spirit is centered rather around honest
inquiry. In this spirit, when I come together with someone from
a completely different subset (and many of the people I know
and love most are from what should be nonintersecting sets),
we can understand each other and come to know each other
precisely because we are concerned about solving the same
aching questions. Inasmuch as we seek together the same aching questions we understand each other, and I think we begin
to make some kind of dent on those questions.

If the agnostic humanist is concerned about the problem of
the "inner cities" and if I, a person who in his eyes was supposed to represent a world in which commitment and freedom of inquiry were mutually exclusive, pursue the same
question with the same frame of mind, each one of us has to
give up our stereotype of the other. And in giving up our
stereotype of the other, a new kind of energy is produced
which we can give to each other and to mankind. This is why
I believe so very much in the principle of nonsegregation.
This does not mean monolith. This does not mean lowest
common denominatorism. It is rather the vitality gained by
mixing a rich diversity of views. I would suggest that it is important for some Catholic students to go to Harvard or

Princeton or Dartmouth or Yale or Brandeis as well as to Notre Dame or Boston College. It is important for them as persons, and perhaps critical for Harvard and Dartmouth and Yale and Brandeis. (With this conviction, I am begging that religious congregations do something about these medieval habits so that we can again assume our citizenship, and that we may, on the free and open market, again volunteer to make our investment in the mainstream of American society.) You see, I would maintain that Harvard and Dartmouth and Yale and Brandeis and Mount Holyoke, my friends, cannot do without some of us. It is just too easy for them without some of us!

A great atheistic friend of mine said: "My God, Sister J., I want to be around places like M.I.T. and Harvard when your generation of theists moves in!" But I am hauntingly aware that this is not an easy kind of involvement. I am hauntingly aware that when one does believe in the open society, when one does believe in involvement, when one does believe in inquiry, one is always taking the chance of losing as much as one gains. I am hauntingly aware that if we make this kind of investment, if we keep making it, some of us are going to get lost, and some of what we believe in is going to be lost. And because I am becoming more and more convinced of the finiteness of my own mind and of my own spirit, we may not even know for sure whether what we lost was absolutely right or absolutely wrong or something in between.

But I would suggest for my own subset that unless we are willing to do this we have just given up the values which we think we own. As long as an intellectual and a seeking society can see us as those people with blinders (physical blinders for some poor nuns who drive, but intellectual and spiritual blinders as well) they can dismiss us easily. But if we really believe in truth, and if we believe we have finite minds, then it seems to me that those of us who believe in what I call the grace life, the supernatural life—if we believe in it and are not phony—ought to be the most courageous or most foolhardy people in the history of mankind. We ought to see the grace life as a new power drive. We ought to see this as a quality which can allow us to go in where others may fear to go.

It's amusing but terrifying to come as a nun to a place like Boston. It is frustrating to walk through the Treadway Hotel and to have the lovely little guy with the Irish brogue who's pushing the go-cart say to you "Are you alone, Sister?" And you say "Yes, I'm alone." He counters with "Is it all right for you to be alone?" and you want to say to him "You know, lad, I'm past nineteen."

But then you know that you and all that you stand for have asked for this kind of image. You have allowed the world community to think of nuns as the cloistered, protected, kind of perpetual intellectual adolescents who have to be sheltered. And yet I spent my life for a principle. I spent my life for a life, a life which I read with my finite mind in the Gospel of a Christ who could make the woman of the Pharisees and the woman of the well and the woman taken in adultery completely at home when they were not at home with anybody else. And I think we have to live with that. We have to decide whether or not we shall become the most empathic, the most compassionate, the most understanding, the most profound people, or the most sheltered. This I would apply to institution after institution in human living. You, I think, have a tremendous responsibility. You represent magazines which for various kinds of subculture groups are at least filtered through as indoctrination. If I could apply for a job I think I would apply for a job with one of the woman's magazines. Not because they are the most acceptably prestigious but because they are working with what I think is one of the toughest markets in the United States, the American suburbanite woman.

The degree of shallowness of mind of so many American suburbanite women terrifies me. Because I believe in a series of approximations, because I believe in bite-size learning, if I were running an American woman's magazine I would really use all my imagination to push that frontier by inches. I would bother her a little, then I would bother her a little more, and then I would bother her a little more. I would work to get that area of gray wider and wider and wider. I would take the chance of overshooting a few times to make sure that I was not undershooting. I would do this for two reasons. First, because I would believe that I had a life to invest in humanity and that was even more important than making money. Then I would be sheerly pragmatic enough, also, to believe that if I would run this to the hilt, I would not have to worry about my stockholders, because I would have one of the most dynamic, one of the most controversial, one of the most alive periodicals around. This is the principle we have operated on with a little unknown college in the Midwest.

It is perfectly understandable to me that when I walk into this kind of a group, some of you very tenderly say to me "Where is Webster?" I must expect this because I come from an institution which is thought of by many as "one of those nuns' colleges" in the United States. They even call us parochial. But to a few people now around this country, a few powerful people, almost too much is expected of us, because these people are convinced that we are already beyond the critical change point, and that we will emerge, within five or six years, as one of the forces of American society.

Little by little we inched on an institution in the last five or six years. Little by little, with a principle. At this point, on the faculty of my college, about forty per cent are Sisters of Loretto who have been educated at a variety of religious and secular institutions. About sixty per cent are lay teachers, and over half of them are not Catholic. They are Jews, every label of Protestant, and some secular humanists.

In mid-May of this year we had one of the most extraordinary days in which I have ever participated. We had a panel which worked with our entire faculty and about twenty of our students who had been invited. On the panel were Dr. Brunner of Harvard, who I think would classify himself a secular humanist; Dr. Elting Morrison, an M.I.T. historian who describes his great-grandfather as "the quasi-pope of the Unitarian Church in New England in 1838"; Father Carroll Stuhmuller, a religious-order priest who is one of the liberal scripture scholars in our church. I was the moderator. All day we addressed ourselves to the question "How do you prepare a student in a college like ours for full participation in the late twentieth century?" Not "How do you protect his faith?" but "How to prepare a student in a college like ours for full participation in the late twentieth century?" How do you get him ready to work next to a Hindu, a secular humanist, a Quaker, a John Bircher? How do you get him ready to work next to them, attempting to solve by successive approximations the problems of race, of population, of economic growth, of all of these things which have profound social implications?

We would suggest that you get him ready only if you subject him to the real pressure of inquiry rather than indoctrination.

This challenge extends to your world. It is good, then, that we have magazines representing different political and philosophic points of view. But none of you can stoop to indoctrinate from your point of view. No one of us, from a vested point of view, can afford to be closed, can afford to indoctrinate. I am a committed Christian, but my commitment to Christianity today is much more dependent on my attempting *not* to proselytize, *not* to indoctrinate, because I happen to believe Christianity is too important to sell so cheaply. I think each one of us must begin again to get this kind of habit of mind, this kind of habit of spirit. It is not easy to live this way.

You are the exponents, I think, of continuing education. You control the market. If the ladies in suburbia read anything, they read *Time, McCall's,* and *The Ladies' Home Journal,* and *Look* and *Life,* and *Better Homes and Gardens.* These often constitute their only continuing education. If you leave them in a narrow ghetto, if you leave them with a lot of pat, glib answers, you are supporting their little narrow world. If you have the courage to keep inching the tension along and to create a highly sophisticated learning mode, then I think what some of us are trying to do in curricular development in the schools is carried on. There may be a new kind of potential alliance here.

These are the thoughts, highly personal I suppose, because only personal convictions are worth anything, that I would like to share with you. If I have a reincarnated life, I shall come and apply to one of you for a job, and would hope I get it.

*. . . the evidence is all around us that the first glimmers of
hope, the first tastes of freedom and self-determination have a
power to release the spirit within a nation, a people, a school
district, a single teacher or a single child.*

Commencement Address
Harris Teachers College
June 15, 1967

Both patterns of history and common sense tell us that grass-
roots revolutions occur not at points of utter hopelessness but
rather when conditions are actually becoming better. Perhaps
this reality gives us one of our most sensitive insights into the
human spirit. The oppression of indoctrination and of fear can
numb and seriously retard the development of a nation, of a
people, of a school district, or of a single teacher or a single
child. Yet the evidence is all around us that the first glimmers
of hope, the first tastes of freedom and self-determination
have a power to release the spirit within a nation, a people, a
school district, a single teacher or a single child.

We watch today the trouble and tension of the struggle of
peoples everywhere to achieve some power over their destinies. We know the anxiety of the day-to-day shifts in the bal-
ance of power between the two great world powers, Soviet

Russia and the United States of America. We know, at the same time, that the power-force of each of these giants somewhat determines the developing destinies of new and old emerging nations. The new Israel, forged out of the centuries of oppression of a people who simply would not yield to genocide of the human spirit; the old Arab states whose new generations of the masses have yet to catch the glimmer of hope that can spark the internal revolutions to reshape the Arab world and the Middle East itself; conflicting energies and yet-to-be released energies in Vietnam and India, in Nigeria and in South Africa: all of these and many more are caught to some degree between peaceful coexistence and the struggle for "secure supremacy" of today's two great powers. But statesmen in Moscow and in Washington today as well as their delegates at the United Nations are vividly aware that they too are caught in the interlocking complexities of the struggles toward self-determination of all the Davids in a Goliath world. Emperors and princes of earlier centuries closed their eyes to this reality, refused to share in creating a new world order. In so doing, they released the future to the revolutionaries whose newly created worlds denied the divine right of kings and thus destroyed the arrogantly naïve security of what seemed to be overwhelming power.

American citizens today proudly point to the pioneer spirit of only two centuries ago, the bootstraps initiative of the frontier. But it is difficult for the economically powerful descendents of those pioneers to remember that the nation was conceived and born in revolution. It was conceived and born out of the misery and the new-found hope and power emerging from a polyglot of religious zealots, escaped prisoners, oppressed peasants, bawdy seamen, and intellectual liberals who somehow saw the potential of the resources of the new land, conceived the American dream, and revolted against the *status quo.* The new era of law and liberty would know the ambiguity of lawlessness and the vice of crusading virtue.

A curriculum project for elementary social studies less than a decade ago proposed the showing of French movies dealing with a different approach to the cowboy-and-Indian theme in our public schools. The French version made the Indians more virtuous than the cowboys. The leaders in the project were convinced, however, that the public school system at that time would never allow this kind of conflicting evidence to disturb the security of patriotic American history.

Only in your lifetime have social-political-economic histories of our own nation begun to be written clearly, confronting us with the reality of the moral and ethical grayness of our past. Our economic order and our political democracy are built on a foundation of extraordinary human initiative and stamina, but the foundation also includes the rotted building materials of Indian and Negro slavery.

If Americans in general and white Americans in particular are to avoid at all the naïve arrogance of emperors and kings, we must, I submit, at this moment in time find the courage and the humility to assess our past with honest eyes.

If the citizenry of United States is to share in and help produce the national revolution within its own borders, and the international revolution in which we are inevitably involved, we must begin to learn and to teach the ambiguities of our own history and the grayness of our own moral virtue as persons and as a people. If the arrogance of power is to avoid destroying not only our vitality but ourselves, we must learn with our students what it is to be a finite, fallible man in finite time; what it is to be a finite, fallible nation at a given finite time in history. Only the courage to face ourselves and our national history clearly can tear from us the blinders of arrogance which impair our vision and harden our hearts as we witness and condemn and attempt to stem the tide of today's revolutionaries.

Of course, both the *sabras* of Israel and the teeming masses of Egypt and Syria have mixed motives and sometimes questionable means of achieving their ends. Like us—and our ancestors—they are fallible finite men struggling to make a more hope-filled future. Of course, the hippie communities of Haight-Ashbury and the peaceniks of Central Park are sometimes naïve and often inconsistent in their proposed solutions and in their functional living. Like us—and our ancestors —they are fallible, finite men struggling to make a more hope-filled future. Of course, Stokely Carmichael and his black-power activists are redressing specific wrongs in seemingly simplistic and violent ways. Like us—and our ancestors—they are fallible finite men struggling to make a more hope-filled future for themselves and their children, whom we and our ancestors simplistically and violently ignored and oppressed.

Revolutions are never orderly. Revolutions produce periods of anarchy or cause new laws and new legal systems. The arms race which many of our citizens see as the only "defense for democracy" could, we all know, produce the world anarchy of nuclear chaos. The political tensions in the back rooms and the corridors of the United Nations are more immediately frightening when they erupt in the chamber of the Security Council and the General Assembly. Once overt and articulated, these tensions will either force us to create new laws and new legal systems to redress the oppressions of earlier finite, fallible laws and legal systems; or they will force us to man the battle stations for the Utopian dream of our past and yield the future to the raw courage and ruthlessness of the new revolutionaries.

Revolutionary persons and nations open up to the future of

man the Pandora's box of hope and new aspirations. As revolutionary persons or nations become the new and responsible authorities in national or world power, they prudently and understandably try to put the lid *they* have lifted back on the box lest the potent energies released destroy them and the world of their finite, fallible dreams.

I do not propose to you a new formula which can restore order to the world. I beg, however, that you as American and world citizens, that you as beginning teachers and, please God, continuing learners, have the courage and the humility to face up to and live with your personal and national limitations. Only so can you possibly face and respect the limitations of other persons and other nations, yield the smugness and the arrogance of power, and share in the evolutionary search to make a future out of the past.

Because much has been done in the past decade to open up our cities, our school systems, our nation, and our world, you are entering the teaching field at a time of almost inevitable continuing tension and revolution. Many will say that the new movements are trying to destroy the past or at least that they fail to acknowledge the great gains of the past. Many will say we are moving too far and too fast. The learning process in our classrooms or in our social order is always more orderly in a world in which teacher and pupil respect and accept the teacher's word for it. The learning process in a community of searchers in a classroom or in a social order is fraught with insecurity and charged with the possibility of really creative breakthrough. The social order, I believe, is day by day more cast in the breakthrough world of search. If the classrooms of the public schools are in synchronization with that style, you and your students will indeed be engaged in education for citizenship. Your loyalty oath to the United States will be a pledge to the future—a pledge to make a little more honest and clear-sighted the finite, fallible, and often fuzzy attempts of those who went before us, so that those who come after us will go on from there.

III   *The Ecumenical World of Search*

The ecumenical world of search is an alternating current, a two-way, many-way street.

—November, 1965

. . . unless you question the existence of God—question, not doubt it—you are a liar or a fool, a fool at least in the apostolic sense, because you have to communicate with a world that is questioning His existence.

Dean's Assembly
Webster College
November 4, 1963

Some time ago a very terrifying statement appeared in a national magazine:

> It is not too much to say that whoever wishes to become a truly moral human being must divorce himself from all the prohibitions, crimes and hypocrisies of the Christian Church. If the concept has any validity or use it can only be to make us larger, freer and more loving. If God cannot do this, then it is time to get rid of him.

The article, a little later, picks up another thread:

> Neither civilized reason or Christian love would cause any of these people to treat you as they presumably wanted to be treated. Only the fear of your power of retaliation would cause them to do that or to seem to do it.

The quotations came from the November 17, 1962, issue of *The New Yorker;* it was, for me, one of the most sobering reading experiences I have had in my life. It was an article called "In a Region of My Mind," the article that really thrust James Baldwin into American literary notice. If you do not recognize Baldwin, you had better recognize him, because he is one of the most literate, one of the most powerful, one of the most provocative, one of the most terrifying young writers of our time; and he is speaking for the Negro population.

With that in the background, remember that he said "If the concept has any validity or any use it can only make us larger, freer and more loving," and he says "If God cannot do this then it is time that we got rid of him."

Now, I would like to suggest that it is Baldwin in the Negro race, Baldwin in the atheistic world, Baldwin in the Southern stereotype, Baldwin in the suburbs of St. Louis—it is all of these strange people with ideas that terrify us, either because of their radical position or because of their conservative position—that we must somehow come to approach in a larger, freer, more loving way. I would suggest that we do not do this by learning a lot of principles; that we do not do this by staying in our own ghettos, by breathing the same air, by telling each other how great it is to be a Christian; but that we find out how great it is to be a Christian by finding out how terrible it is to be a human being. I am using "terrible" in a wonderful sense of "terrifying," in the realization that there is nobody who grows without going through growing pains, and the growing pains are never over.

So I have said to many leading Catholic educators that I really wonder what would happen if the United States government declared to us tomorrow: "Yes, we will give you the money to run your schools on every level—on the elementary-school level, on the undergraduate level, on the secondary-school level, on the graduate-school level. You can have the money through the parents; you can have it directly through institutions; but as soon as we give it to you, remember that we want you to have equal but *separate* rights."

It seems to me that if the government did this, if the government said to us "Yes, you can have equal but separate rights," we would scream to high heaven. We would remember that that is what we did to the American Negro. We are trying to overcome that separation today because we are clever enough to realize that you do not have an influence on your society unless you are part of the mainstream of that society.

What are you as an individual meant to contribute to the apostolate of the Seventies, Eighties, and Nineties and the Two-thousands? Out there is a world waiting for all of us to communicate with it. Somehow or other we have to be able to begin to understand that world; not to debate with it, not to apologize for our own position by defending it in the old apologia sense; but we have to be able to go into that world and to find out what that world is all about.

I want to quote to you again from probably my favorite Christian writer of this time, Daniel Berrigan, who says:

> When ideas remain too long unexercised, a man who begins as an intellectual, his mind in good trim, ends shapeless of mind, useless of mind.
>
> The fault is that [the Christian] would glory in the history of man or the history of the Church as great ideas; but of his own times would know nothing . . . that a man would not think his own times worth the price of knowing.
>
> And let us not be deceived; the price of the knowledge is a heavy one. The price of knowing one's own times is always, to a Christian, the price of acting on behalf of one's own times. Whereas the knowledge of the past has no price attached to it; it is like the knowledge of the dead; it demands no living risks; neither the risk of misunderstanding nor of estrangement nor of practical mistake.

But to know the living is always a risky process. It implies the risks of knowledge that must itself be living, since it centers on the living; that must be open, since the object of knowledge is an "other," and therefore changing, growing, evading.

[And then he talks about what he calls "the tribal and family optimism which is the death warrant of reality."]

Among Christians of our day [he says] it persists in parochial minds who measure all things by the traditional plumb line—the line which joins a rectory to a school to a series of comfortable interlocked streets. This is the nursery world of the unawakened. Beyond is a terrifying unknown.

And if we come to what we might call the geometry of mystery, the line which joins sacramental experience to human life, we would note a strange parallel to the geography of today's parish.

The invisible line here would run from baptistry to pulpit to altar, and on to school and home. In many Christian lives, it would be a line drawn in early childhood, and hewn to through adulthood—a line which has deepened into a rut. In another sense, it is a line which has become a party line; it joins man to man, the ethical, the cheerful, the interiorly pure, the good suburbanites. As clearly and jealously as a property line, upon which Christian taxes have been paid, and which therefore by the logic of the suburbs must be kept free from squatter man, this line traces for fathers and their children, the limits beyond which the Christian vocation will not go, the limits it has set to its free action. One can be baptized, shrive, take the Eucharist, live and die—and never touch the real world; lead a sectarian, safe, pragmatic life, and call it a religious life; never be troubled about the judgment of God on such a life; never experience anguish over "the world, the way it goes"; never experience the jealousy of God or the silence of God; never waver before the alternatives which mankind holds out—to choose; to renege; to refuse.

As you may guess, I am presently possessed by the wonder and mystery of freedom—possessed as I have never been before by the wonder and mystery of freedom, meditating all the time about the foolishness of God, who knew what it meant to make me free. Who knew that in making me free, He would let me choose. Who knew that in making me free, He could let me succeed or fail. Who was fool enough to let me make a choice even about salvation or damnation. And so it seems to me, if He put such a terrible price on vitality; if He really made such a terrible investment in the grace which He gave to me; then indeed, grace must be the most important thing of the Christian life—the sharing in the divine life of Christ which we call grace. The kind of preoccupation which sees the Christian life as a series of rules and regulations, a series of prescriptions and proscriptions, is a deadening kind of stricture which smothers the force of the grace life in vitality and action.

In this framework I believe that we have to re-evaluate our whole position about the future role of education and the Christian world. We have indeed become at least late-adolescent Catholics, ready and perhaps compulsive about going out and getting involved in the dynamics of our contemporary world. This great aching atheistic and agnostic world is essentially contemplative and is waiting somehow for the vitality that comes out of people who are unafraid to be afraid, who have what I call *the security to be insecure,* who so believe in their faith that they are not afraid to look at all the terrifying aberrations that we see around us. At Brandeis University I said that the image that so many people have of Roman Catholic nuns disturbs me deeply. They think of us as a protected young naïve group, sheltered from the cold winds of reality. Too often even our students somehow get mislead with this kind of notion. In many a high school the advent of a nun into a conversation in process would cause a young student group to change the subject with a kind of embarrassed attitude of "Sister is too young to know."

And yet when we think about it, we are the shock troops of the Church. If we are the guerrilla fighters who decided that it was worth it to put no barriers on our contribution, then it seems to me that we ought to be the most mature people in the world, that we ought to have the best chance of anybody in the whole world of being as comfortable as Christ with the woman at the well, with the woman taken in adultery, and Mary Magdalen; that perhaps the prostitute ought to come into our arms faster than she comes into anybody else's because she trusts us to have gambled for tremendous involvement in the grace life, the divine life which is the Christ life. And it seems to me that if our education is going anywhere that we have to create in our first-line troops this same kind of compassion, this same kind of open heart and open mind in terrifying wonder at God's world so that we will not be like those suburbanites Berrigan talks about, who are secure and who have traced their lines around the Christian property on which Christian taxes have been paid. Rather we will be the people who learn in the experimental process to meet the world and to be undone by it by getting to know people with varying kinds of viewpoints.

My mother and dad told me not long ago about a Protestant couple whose young son came home to our little town with a Master's degree in psychology. He came home to his wonderful provincial atmosphere, sat down at the table, and his mother said to him: "It is your turn to give the grace." And he, who was twenty-two, said: "I don't do that any more." His father and mother were undone, and they came to talk to my father and mother and asked what they should do.

When my mother asked me what to tell them, I said: "Mother, please tell them to be patient with him. Please tell them to love him. Please tell them not to preach to him. Please, somehow or other, ask his parents to give him the great security of whatever is their basic involvement in Christianity so that he can live it out for a while without a terrible guilt complex."

Then I began to talk to my mother about some of my atheistic friends. For the first time in my life I saw my mother afraid. She said to me, in great simplicity, "Don't gamble too much." My mother has never known an atheist . . . not really known one, not really loved one. She never had a chance to say "Who are you?" and I'm sure, because I have the greatest respect for her, that if she ever gets to know one, she is going to be a lot better than I am at saying "Who are you?" I trust her that much. But I will say to you who are not yet twenty-one that you can't afford to let happen to you what happened to my mother, because you have to live in a world of terrible insecurity and even try to get inside. You have to contribute to it, and so you have to have the powerful courage to say to these people: "Who are you?" You have to say it to people of every kind. So I beg you not to defend your faith. I beg you not to engage in arguments with your next date. But I do beg you to live your faith not by getting yourself all inside a nice little network as to what's right and what's wrong, but by developing such an attitude and such a vigor in the grace life through the sacramental system that you can live in terrible insecurity and even try to get inside.

A year and a half ago I had the privilege of attending a two-and-a-half-week conference at M.I.T.'s Endicott House. I was the only Sister and one of five women with a group of about fifty men. I am sure that fifty per cent of the people at that conference were atheistic or agnostic. At the end of the conference one brilliant historian said to me: "Sister, there has been a lot of talk about existence theorems here—but the one existence theorem no one counted on confronting was you. For four days many of us tried to convince ourselves that your freedom of inquiry was phony and for the next four days that your commitment was phony. At the end of the first week nobody could convince himself that either was phony. And all we've got to say is you are damned hard on us."

But I, too, have very few crutches that I once had. There was a time when I was your age and could say blithely "those stupid idiots who can say they believe in the brotherhood of man and not in the fatherhood of God," and I could dismiss them very quickly. I can't do that any more because I know legions of them who think they do not believe in the fatherhood of God and who are living the concept of the brotherhood of man in a way I wish I could. And so I have to rethink this whole process again. I have to keep asking myself every day and every hour: "What does the fatherhood of God mean?" The answers are not cheap, and the quest is rather terrifying. Priests who know some of my views write me letters cynically asking me whether they are liars or fools because they never questioned the existence of God. But I will say to you, who are not yet twenty-one, that unless you question the existence of God—question, not doubt it—you are a liar or a fool, a fool at least in the apostolic sense, because you have to communicate with a world that is questioning His existence.

Every morning when I get up I have to ask the question because I have invested everything that I am and have on that one fact; and if I am wrong, I want to know it. And so if my faith is anything, then my faith is that which can make me more and more mature. And if that faith can communicate with anything or anyone else, then it has to be seen by those people as a living force.

Really mature people are very complex. Really mature people have not learned any simple answers. They are not asking for some kind of safe and secure way in which somebody will always tell them whether they are safe or sorry, whether they are right or wrong. Life is a terribly lonely process.

It is lonely and wonderful and terrifying to find out who you are. You will not find this out in any kind of hermitage or isolation, but you will find it out in confrontation. You will find it out by confronting people of every imaginable kind. And so we are saying that we are ready to try at least one other form of Christian education at Webster College. Not everyone agrees, but there are a growing number of us who are committed to establishing as much dynamic on Webster's campus as we can possibly establish. We have begun to say in print that about fifty per cent of our faculty are lay people, that about fifty per cent of those people are not of our faith, and that some of them are men and women of integrity with no formal, organized religion. In such a community, the reverberations that I as a faculty member and you the students have on our whole wonderful, at least potentially interlocked, world are incredible.

A year and a half ago I sat at dinner at Cambridge with Dr. Bruner and Mr. Walton and a few others. Dr. Bruner, the Harvard psychologist, had heard a good deal about a Webster sophomore. A number of people had said that she was a very exciting student. Bruner said: "I know what we'll do, Sister J. Let's talk to Polly Bunting at Radcliffe about a junior year at Radcliffe for this kind of student from Webster College. My God, think what she would do to Radcliffe!" Now this is very important—not what Radcliffe would do to her but what she would do to Radcliffe.

And at this point Mr. Walton from our faculty said: "Jerry, we forgot to tell you one very important thing. She is joining the Sisters of Loretto this fall."

With this, Dr. Bruner stopped a minute, then said: "I don't think I can fight with that. At this moment I can think of nothing more important than being sure we have that kind of Sister of Loretto in the next generation." Now Bruner hadn't really known a sister a few years ago. He had known *about* them, as I knew *about* atheists and agnostics.

This summer a number of our girls played roles in various kinds of places—some of them were up at M.I.T., one was at the University of Minnesota, a couple of them were in a Kosher Jewish camp. These people and all the rest of the students perhaps, who had experiences that I don't know about, have a tremendous reverberative effect. And I am sure that they came back not as they were before.

A great modern Catholic scripture scholar has said to some of us that it is his personal conviction that an atheist of integrity is in the state of grace. When he said this, I almost jumped up and down, almost climbed the mountains and waved. I who had as a child wondered how eternity could be exciting am now caught up with wonder that God and eternity may indeed be inexhaustible. I have a finite mind and everybody else that has gone along the way had a finite mind, even Thomas Aquinas. I know I'm becoming obnoxious at this point by saying to my philosopher friends "If God, who is omniscient and omnipotent, could create a Thomas why couldn't he create a greater Thomas in the twentieth century and in the twenty-first? And if Thomas had as great a mind as he had, wouldn't he ask new questions in the twentieth century with seven centuries of new data?"

I am awfully interested in finding a way to make students philosophize as well as to know about philosophy. It is this kind of questioning mind that will allow you to communicate with the world and allow the world to communicate with you. If others know you haven't got the world by the tail; if they know that you find the world terrifying but beautiful and interesting and full of wonder, then they will begin to communicate with you. Then I think you will be driven back to the chapel, the Communion table, into the silence of your own heart with completely new kinds of contemplation, with completely new kinds of involvement. The principal question remains: How much do we want to be involved; and are we willing to pay the price?

Newspapers quote me cryptically as having said I no longer would join a Catholic learned society. I say this because I think it is so important that I, as a Catholic, as one of the many Christians, one of the many people self-consciously possessed of the grace life, be involved in the great mainstream of intellectual movements. If there is an American Psychological Association, I can see no reason in the world for establishing a Catholic Psychological Association, but I can see every reason in the world for having Catholics deeply involved in the American Psychological Association.

I want our Catholic students to become involved in professional theater, but I don't want them to get involved in some kind of Catholic theater—because I don't think such a thing exists. There is a magnificent place for someone possessed of the grace life in the theater, in journalism, in mathematics, in physics, in poetry.

And so at the same time I say that I would like to throw out Catholic textbooks. I maintain that I want great textbooks written by Catholics. I want those textbooks to be so good that they could be used at Harvard and Princeton as well as Webster College. We must have persons with the vitality of the grace life who can see history with such insight that their works are chosen to be used in the great educational centers of this country, but not Catholics who write Catholic textbooks with a Catholic point of view for Catholic schools.

I want students to have a real point of view. Perhaps a real point of view will come from conflicting points of view. At the time when students are exposed to the best vitality we can give them, the vitality of a stimulating theology department, I do not want them to waste that time by keeping them sheltered from conflict and diverging viewpoints. I want to use that time to get many conflicting and divergent viewpoints into them and confronting them so that they can *vitally* go back to the vital theology department and use the department in a new way.

And so we like to think that in a few years at least twenty-five per cent of the people sitting in a Webster College assembly will be non-Catholic, because then we would begin to have a greater and greater kind of involvement and inter-dynamics going on. I no longer think it is important for every Catholic student to be in a Catholic school, but I think it is terribly important to have some awfully good Catholic schools —not veneered, not safe, but dynamic kinds of schools which include the Catholic contribution.

Perhaps we can build this kind of institution at Webster College. Perhaps it will be one of the revolutionary stages that will make ready for the great *parousia* of the intellectual life when one day, please God, in a student's lifetime if not in mine, we will see Princeton and Harvard and Illinois and Michigan and Berkeley running to admit the great Christian intellectuals, because the major colleges will see them as such intellectually dynamic people, careful but not cautious!

Today, November 4, 1963, is the fifth anniversary of the coronation of Pope John. There is a coincidence. This morning's gospel for the feast of St. Charles Borromeo told the story of the talents. (It is that awful gospel that stops before it really gets to the point.) It talks about the man who had ten talents, and the man who had five, and then it tells about the man who had one and went and buried it. It never tells you what happened to the man who buried his talent. I would like to finish the Bible story for you:

"But he who had received the one talent came and said, 'Master, I know that thou art a stern man; thou reapest where thou hast not sowed and gatherest where thou hast not winnowed; and as I was afraid, I went away and hid thy talent in the earth; behold, thou hast what is thine.' But his master answered and said to him, 'Wicked and slothful servant!' "

Now if you go and follow that gospel narrative into the next chapters you will find the narrative about the separation of the sheep and goats. And this account is a springboard into another link which I had never discovered before. It is that lovely passage in the gospel that says: "I was hungry and you gave me to eat. I was thirsty, I was naked. I was sick. I was in prison and you came to me."

Those who came to the sick and hungry and those in prison were the sheep. The others who were afraid of the hungry, the thirsty, the naked, the sick, and avoided those in prison were the goats.

And you remember He said to them: "As long as you did it for one of these, the least of my brethren, you did it for me." And you know how it ends. It says: "Enter into the joy of everlasting life."

The everlasting life is beginning at this minute. We are already in eternity. Eternity is just a continuance of the divine life we live now. And how did He say you are going to have it? You are going to have it if you go to the hungry and thirsty and the naked and the sick, and those in prison. And this means all the people who don't understand you until you understand them.

We who are the apostles, we who are the shock troops of the Church, we who are the guerrilla fighters of the grace life, must plunge into that other world and find out what makes that world go, so that we can vitalize it and be vitalized by it.

This is what I would like to cry to students and people all over the world, because I think we can't wait for it much longer. I would like to say it first or share it first or confront first with it our own students, who belong to our own college at this moment in time. We cannot afford to be slothful. We cannot afford to be safe. But we must afford to be involved in the magnificent dynamic of faith that is secure enough to be insecure, in the real kind of detachment, humility, and dependence that says:

"I live with His life; and I run with it."

We are lying to ourselves, we are lying to each other, we are lying to the public, if we maintain that the grace of a vocation can make up for conditions which of themselves make the teachers ineffectual. Each of us in our religious formation learned that the definition of supernatural implies that which is above the natural and not that which is contrary to it!

Archdiocesan Council of Catholic Men
St. Louis
April 1, 1962

Records available to me show that approximately 127,000 students are enrolled in the St. Louis archdiocesan secondary and elementary schools this year. At an average cost per student of $500, which is *under* the public school average in the greater metropolitan St. Louis area, this means that the Catholic population is contributing through tuition, through the endowed lives of teaching religious, through philanthropic support—and, we must admit, even through substandard salaries—at least $60 million per year to subsidize the educational expenditures of the metropolitan taxpayers.

Since I represent one of the principal subsidizing groups, the nonsalaried teaching Sisters, I have made a great personal investment in the enterprise which is Catholic education. And you, as contributors to your parishes and to expansion fund drives, continue to make a varied and important contribution.

Precisely because we have made and continue to make these contributions, it seems to me that we must continually reappraise the reason for the investment, the strengths and weaknesses of the results at this time, the power of these results to gain greater understanding and support. Only through this kind of inquiring concern can we assume a valid and healthy position in the general misunderstanding which has arisen over the aid-to-education controversy.

Let us look first at the strengths of Catholic education in the St. Louis area at this time. Some 20,000 students are now in private secondary schools or archdiocesan high schools in the area. It can be said with conviction that each of these schools now meets the requirements of both the State of Missouri and the North Central Association with regard to faculty status, class size, and facilities. To accomplish this step, all of us know, has not been easy. There remain, as we all know, a number of Catholic students who are not in Catholic high schools. Still, we have the assurance that in the field of secondary education we are meeting our obligation, in justice, at least "reasonably well." We have assumed the responsibility of maintaining the secondary schools; in so doing we have assumed the responsibility of teaching social studies, language arts, mathematics, science, foreign languages, fine arts, and all the other important disciplines. But only if we find the resources in money, in facilities, in teaching personnel to meet all these challenges in secondary education have we the right to continue to discharge this responsibility. Were we to assume that we could keep these people in secondary schools of substandard quality so that we might assure the students of catechetical instruction, this instruction would be a hypocrisy and a farce. May the press of numbers never lead us into this kind of snare.

In the field of higher education in the St. Louis area, Catholic institutions and Catholic support have made great contributions. St. Louis University, and the three women's colleges—Fontbonne, Maryville, and Webster—each owned and operated by a religious congregation, have all been approved for many decades by the leading accrediting associations. Each is faced at the present time with tremendous challenges. Every college and university administrator knows that a worthwhile professor ten years from now will require a salary double that which he is now getting; each administrator knows that he must accomplish tremendous strides in quantity and quality of resources if he is to maintain his institution in justice in the field of higher education in the next decade. And so each of us must calmly and coolly face the issue that we will meet these challenges or we will, in order to satisfy justice, withdraw from this phase of the educational endeavor. I do not say this lightly! Again, I believe that only if we are true to our responsibility in that professional field which we have assumed, can we be true to our Catholic apostolate in that field. Were we to maintain substandard colleges and universities in order that post-teenagers get further catechetical instruction, we would indeed be sounding brass and tinkling cymbal. If we can maintain these institutions so that maturing and questioning young minds may integrate tough theological formation into vital intellectual struggles, then indeed ours is a great contribution to the community.

When we look at the third great unit of our Catholic education continuum and perhaps the most important of them all—the elementary school—the picture is not so clear. That the efforts have been great no one can question. That these efforts have produced *acceptable results* we must indeed question. But there is hope for the future even as it reassures us that there is need for improvement. As the network that is our elementary school system is drawn into an administrative unity; as we have for the first time a school board related to the archdiocesan office, which can work toward regulation of class size and faculty qualifications, we are at least moving in the right direction. Perhaps this is as courageous a move on the part of our Cardinal as was another very courageous move which he made in the early days of integration of the schools.

If the archdiocesan schools and the school board are to get the kind of support and cooperation they will unquestionably need in the coming decade, the people in the parishes must very clearly and coldly face the facts of our elementary schools as they exist today. The size of most of the classes is appalling. There remains a great number of undegreed teachers who, through misguided zeal, are making a negative rather than a positive contribution to our schools. A process by which graduates of our high schools are lured into parochial schoolteaching under the guise of apostolic zeal, rather than invited to prepare themselves so that they may justly and fruitfully contribute to the formation of young minds in the future, must be cut off. Here, indeed, the press of numbers has led us into many snares. Last year, five girls who failed to meet our standards for readmission after first or second year at Webster College obtained jobs in parochial schools. Every year, high school graduates with both money and ability to pursue college educations withdraw applications in order to accept positions as teachers of your children. There have been courageous moves on the part of some people to escape this dilemma. Chief among the courageous have been the mothers general of many of the teaching orders represented in the St. Louis area. Many of these orders were among the first to establish houses of studies in which their young sisters finish their college educations and receive their bachelor's degrees before ever stepping into the classroom to accept the responsibility of educating your children. In making the decision to establish these houses of studies, each of these mothers general knew that she was cutting off the supply of teaching sisters to her missions for at least two years. She knew also that she was assuming a financial burden for her community for which she had no means of incoming support. Still, she knew that if she was to meet in justice the apostolate which her community had undertaken in the field of education, she could not compromise in the preparation of these teaching sisters. Therefore, she sacrificed what looked like immediate goods for the longer-range gain which was needed to fulfill her obligation.

This first step has been taken. Still these teaching sisters must go into schools in which many of the lay faculty, because of substandard salaries, do not meet the sisters' qualifications. Still these sisters must attempt to teach in classrooms in which the numbers make their roles much more those of babysitters than formers of vital young minds. We are lying to ourselves, we are lying to each other, we are lying to the public if we maintain that the grace of a vocation can make up for conditions which of themselves make the teachers ineffectual. Each of us in our religious formation learned that the definition of supernatural implies that which is above the natural and not that which is contrary to it!

I am saddened that even the courageous Father Curtin must say that we are aiming at a top size of forty-nine for our elementary classrooms. This, I personally submit, is not radical enough to allow us to fulfill our obligation in justice. And so you will say to me "What is the answer?"—and I will say to you "I do not know," but I do know some criteria upon which we must find the answer. To assume the responsibility of fulfilling any important professional role within a Catholic agency, we must assure ourselves of the resources to meet the demands of that professional role in justice. I am sure that we would all readily agree that to operate a Catholic hospital with unqualified medical staff and inadequate facilities would be a blunder against prudence precisely because it would be a blunder against justice. Our Catholic hospitals, and even our Catholic higher education institutions, have received a continuing increase of public understanding. This understanding has developed as the public at large realizes that the first goal of the administrations of these schools, these hospitals, is for professional excellence, and that their Catholic philosophy undergirds and supports this commitment to professional excellence in their own field. The support has *not* been given because these institutions claim to be saving the taxpayer from further expenditures!

All of this, I suggest, has a very important bearing on the general misunderstanding which surrounds the aid-to-education controversy today. Whether or not you support or oppose federal aid to education is not the question. Whether or not you support or oppose any kind of public aid to private education is, of course, a question. It is a question which has constitutional implications, procedural implications, as well as implications of interpretation and timing. I personally suggest that we *were* ready and *are* ready to work toward public support for higher education precisely because we have begun to establish the image of making a strong professional contribution for the national and local community. I think we shall soon be ready to interpret our case for secondary education precisely because we have proved our commitment to professional standards and have not fallen into the trap of maintaining protective catechetical centers in which we do as much in professional fields as our limitations will allow. I personally do not feel that we are ready to interpret our case for elementary education. We will be ready to do this when, and only when, we can show the public at large that we are asking them to support a system which is committed not only in theory, but also in real practice to professional standards which are second to none. If, instead, we simply show them a weakened system which is content to exist with standards that would not meet accreditation, we are strengthening their image of us as a Sunday School that conducts its classes from Monday through Friday. I am well aware of the consequences of this kind of evaluation. There are many who with great conviction maintain that the only way that we can overcome these deficiencies is by gaining public support. I simply believe that we cannot, and perhaps should not, get this support until we have earned a different image.

There is, of course, an irony involved in all of this. To achieve these kinds of standards without public support requires one of two courses of action. The first would be an even greater sacrifice on the part of our Catholic constituency to summon the resources in money and in personnel to achieve the standards which would be acceptable to the public and even to ourselves. This *perhaps* is impossible. The second course would be to accept as inevitable the fact that we cannot educate even as great a ratio of Catholic students as we now house in our schools. If the first course—further support for growth in professional excellence—is impossible, then I vote for the second course of action. I vote for it for two reasons. First, because I believe it is the just answer. It would mean that we would have to establish strong and vital catechetical centers in which creative new forces would find creative new ways to integrate tough theological formation into the secularized education which these young people would be receiving, but it would also mean that those elementary schools which are maintained under Catholic auspices would emerge as professionally excellent, as a demonstration of the vitality which can come from a truly integrated educational formation. It is my personal opinion that even a cutback in quantity here would allow us to produce a quality which would begin to earn and to get the kind of public understanding which will one day give us the public support necessary to implement the contribution which our Catholic community will continue to make to the community at large.

I am fascinated by a statement made by the courageous Father Theodore Hesburgh, the president of Notre Dame University. Father Hesburgh has said: "Ours it is to be a bridge and a beacon and not a ghetto in our society." Each of us and all of us must meditate on this phrase: we must search for ways that we can implement this kind of thinking in all fields of our apostolate, but particularly in the field of education; whether it be at the college, the secondary, or the elementary level. The worst mistake we could make at this time would be to oversimplify the issues. Our educators, our pastors, our parents, and even our students must brood over the issues, must seek creative and productive answers for the future—answers based not in compromise but in justice.

There is no direction in which we will not look.

Xavier University Forum
Cincinnati, Ohio
November, 1965

I have a passion for the open society of multiple alternatives and it is about that open society I want to talk.

The world of transportation and communication and technology which we have all inherited and which we all go on making has made it impossible for any person in any situation to live inside a closed system. It is impossible for national groups to live in isolation. It is impossible for socioeconomic groups to live in isolation. It is impossible for racial groups to live or be forced to live in isolation. And in that sense I think we have again been freed to become more contemplative.

This development in the history of mankind has emerged at the same time that the whole process of democratic rule has begun to transform civilization. Think a little bit about the very tiny timeline that has been the timeline of the democratic process. Except for that very short interlude which did not persist, the interlude of the Greek states, we have had really only about two centuries, a tiny two hundred years on a timeline of perhaps some two million or perhaps twenty million years of the existence of the world. Only two hundred years to begin to test our wings. Only two hundred years to begin to make our social institutions, our religious institutions, our political institutions, our philosophical systems come to terms with the democratic process.

I want to suggest to you that the democratic process, not for its preservation but for its evolution, is totally dependent on at least two important characteristics. One is the ongoing development of the ability to make personal decisions. I am firmly convinced that democracy cannot be sustained and cannot go forward (and unless it goes forward it will not be sustained) without giving to all persons not only the right but also the growing ability, the growing practice in personal, lonely decision-making.

The second criterion on which I think democracy stands is a continuing respect for the due process of law. The due process of law is the guardian, the protector, the insurance policy of personal decision-making. The polar world of a police state provided for us Nazi Germany—Nazi Germany where, under the pale of Western Christendom, our people gave up their free minds and free will to such an extent that they tolerated and allowed the destruction of six million Jews. We live in a world today which is just beginning to wake up to the travesty of racial segregation in the most free land that ever existed—the travesty of unequal rights in a world that is trying to find its way. Our society is trying to find its way out of guilt into new creative processes so that it can begin to act on the belief that all men are precious personal individuals. I would fight and bleed and die for the right and the obligation of a man to make personal decisions. I would fight and bleed and die for the preservation of due process of law and for the learning of due process of law in many of our institutions, including the Church, which have not yet learned that process.

I sat in Washington a few weeks ago at the Arena Theatre and watched Shaw's *Joan of Arc*. I watched that play with interest, with great empathy. If any of you have seen that play, I think you will agree with me that it has no villain. The English lord is not a villain; the Cardinal is not a villain; the grand inquisitor is not a villain, the Dauphin is not a villain, the soldiers are not villains, Joan is not a villain. But each of them is trying to protect a system somewhere. Each is trying to protect a vested interest. Each is fighting for his little piece and guarding that little piece, terribly afraid to let a free voice speak out. The epilogue of the play is a beautiful, lyrical thing. Shaw lets Joan come back and pounce on the Dauphin's bed and say "Is it right that they've made me a saint? Really, is it right that they've made me a saint?" And he convinces her. "Yes, yes, they've vindicated you, they've made you a saint." And one by one each of the people who helped persecute her comes back on the stage so happy that they've made her a saint. Then someone suggests: "What if we ask God to bring her back?" And one by one they leave the stage and say, "My God, no."

I think we all feel a little like that. I feel like that as a college president. I'm sure the mother of a family sometimes feels like that. Because freedom is a terrifying thing. Freedom means that we have the ability to make terrible mistakes. We have the ability to be imprudent. There is no such thing as freedom only to be prudent. There is no such thing as freedom only to be conservative. There is no such thing as freedom only to agree with me.

One of the loveliest anecdotes I've ever heard is said to have taken place at one of the seminaries in the United States. The liberal theologian Hans Kung was to speak. And it is told that the bulletin board carried the sign: "All are required to hear Father Kung's lecture on freedom." We need to laugh a little at this kind of situation because we desperately need to keep our sense of humor. Only our sense of humor will protect us from becoming cynical as we begin to vote for the freedom and responsibility to take the weight of our own actions on our own shoulders. Moral responsibility is the ability to respond to a moral situation which is never unilateral, which is never monolithic, which is always freighted with many facets.

I want to discuss more fully the three writers who have had a great influence on me. I am told by my friends that writers who have an influence on me are those in whom I recognize myself. I do not apologize for that, because I believe that is what we should do. I think we should go into life and get ideas and test those ideas against great minds. We should never follow the Pied Piper of Hamlin, be he theologian, statesman, or philosopher.

One of the men in whom I recognized a little piece of myself is Karl Rahner, the great Jesuit theologian philosopher, who wrote *The Christian Commitment* in which he develops his diaspora theme. Rahner says that the Jews left Jerusalem and dispersed all over the then modern world and were the Jews of the diaspora. Rahner suggests that we are now Christians in a diaspora. We have moved out of the Christian West in a diaspora. Christianity is reduced and exalted to the Christian grace about which I am self-reflective and you are self-reflective, the Christian grace that is translated into every secular institution in civilization today. Rahner says that this is the kind of a civilization into which we are retreating when we try to set up Christian social service or Christian education or Christian art. Rather today we must be Christians in education, Christians in art, Christians in social culture. This is a tough attitude for your president and me to examine dispassionately when we have multimillion-dollar investments in brick and mortar at Webster College and Xavier University.

The second person whose thought I would like to weave into my remarks is probably the one who has had the most profound influence on my own thinking. He is another Jesuit, Teilhard de Chardin, the paleontologist, philosopher and humanist who develops his theory of evolution: a biological evolution but also spiritual and social evolution. Chardin suggests that we are at the babyhood of mankind. He suggests that when evolution reached the point of self-reflective man, man took the responsibility for what I would call the vector force of evolution. Man took the responsibility for both the direction and the rate at which this civilization should continue to evolve. We live in a very, very open world. We live in a world which is dividing itself into the tradition-oriented world, fighting for the systematization which somebody put together at one time, and the evolutionary focused world, which is always looking to push back the frontiers of what we know.

My mother and father graced me with life. They graced me with biological life about forty years ago when they conceived me in an act of love. My mother and father graced me again last weekend when that lovely farm couple from Illinois, who have been married fifty-one and a half years, talked with me about Rahner, about Chardin, about Harvey Cox and about the ecumenical world in which we live. Somehow or other my mother and father gave us the power to be ourselves. And so I have moved out of a society that they know about, and yet I have not moved out of the ken of their understanding. I discussed with my mother and father one of the toughest problems of my life, and they sat and said at seventy-four and

seventy-two: "The only thing we have ever asked of you, and
the only thing we shall ever ask of you is to be honest." And
they meant that. They meant that to their toes. They meant it
not in words; they meant it in deeds. They will never retract
that from us operationally. They gave us the freedom to be
free. And so they have given us a sense of terrible responsibility.

Chardin, in what he calls *The Future of Man*, suggests that
those of us who are interested in the future-oriented world see
the ripples of the future in the patterns of the past. We are
beginning to be a new community, maybe a new mystical
body, whether it be called Christians, Jews, Hindus, or Agnostics. Some of us are contemplative about the future, and believe that truth is not a platonic mass somehow put together
by a man named Thomas never to be tampered with again.
Some of us really believe that it is always ours to make a new
synthesis which will disintegrate to become a new synthesis
which will disintegrate to make a new synthesis. Those of us
can always live in an ecumenical world of search.

Persons are at their worst when they argue with one another. But persons are at their very best when they admit that
they know a little bit, and that there is a heaven of a lot more
to know. We get to live for twenty or forty or sixty or maybe
ninety years, and we get to run to and through our graves
finding out a little bit and leaving the rest to these wonderful
kids who are going to live behind us. They are twenty, a precious twenty. They have a nineteen-year lead on me because
they're twenty in the post-John XXIII world. They're twenty
at a time when we've really begun to take down the barriers.
They've got nineteen years to catch up to my chronological
age, and if they're not a lot better than I am when they're
thirty-nine, I'm a mess, and so are you.

If we believe in an evolutionary world, we want student

protests. If we believe in an evolutionary world, we want student skepticism. If we believe in an evolutionary world, we want student disagreement because student freedom implies student imprudence. If we are going to have student creativity, we must tolerate a world in which somebody burns his draft card. We must tolerate that world whether or not we agree with his burning his draft card. Perhaps that is not the decision that we could make in a given situation, but if we create a world in which nobody can make that "mistake" in our estimation, we have begun to move toward the world of the police state. My greatest defense for this position is that it is the position of almighty God. Almighty God, my theologian friends have told me since I learned the Baltimore Catechism, gave me free will. He really gave me free will. And I was told that to create a moral act called sin, I had to have sufficient reflection and full consent of the will. To be really virtuous, I have to have sufficient reflection and full consent of the will. At least I must approximate those qualities if I am to be capable of great acts. Almighty God knew that you could commit murder, and almighty God knew that you could create an act of great compassion. Almighty God knew that you could create an act of terrible judgment upon a fellow human being, and he also knew that you could sympathize with him. But he so put a price on freedom that He allowed this terribly messy world.

I gave a lecture to our freshmen a couple of years ago, and I was talking on this business of freedom, as I shall always talk on it. I said to them: "Let's consider the behavior of a puppet, the behavior of a Rockette, and the behavior of a creative dancer. It is possible that every one of these beings could do the same thing with his right hand at the same time. The puppet would be manipulated by the mechanical apparatus of the puppeteer. The Rockette would be manipulated by her prior desire to stay in the chorus line and to follow the directions of the choreographer. But the creative dancer would be controlled only by the limits of her own creativity. Is the creative dancer undisciplined? Is the creative dancer less disciplined than the puppet? Is the creative dancer less disciplined than the Rockette? I don't think so. But the discipline is inside the individual, structured in the individual with her response to what it is she wants to do."

It is the discipline that must inform the moral choice made by every concerned, compassionate man who makes fallible decisions with consequences for other men, the power and the discipline to act when one cannot clearly see the consequences of one's choice.

But we are infinitesimally powerful because we will either be a nonimportant, nondirected person in a society, or we will be a lever force in a society. In my estimation, we will be a lever force only if we are true to ourselves, only if we take the responsibility of our own decisions on ourselves. Does this mean that we throw away tradition? Does this mean that we throw away dogma, that we throw away history? No. It means simply that there is no question that we will not examine and re-examine. It means simply that there is no direction in which we will not look. It means simply that some day no sister or no seminarian will ever be refused the right to read anything or listen to anybody. Because if we believe in truth, we are not afraid of the search for it. If we believe that God loves us, then we believe that the human being must be competent to deal with truth and with error.

In this sense, the process of education is preparing people for a democratic society. It is not an education to facts but the process that teaches people to learn to learn.

In what library could scientists find the way to launch the satellites? The blueprint was not there.

When I was a freshman in college I went to a football game in St. Louis. Half of us left the stands and went out to the parking lot to stand in a long line to wait our turn to get inside a little trailer. We spent half the football game waiting for our chance to get inside the little trailer because inside was a box called a television set into which we were told they were beaming that football game. I, who love football, had left the game to stand in the cold line. I walked out of that trailer, and I made a complete ass of myself. I said to my friends, and they'll never let me forget it: "That's very interesting, but they'll never get it across town." I thank God, and I thank myself for my stupidity; it was such a grandiose mistake that I think it set me on a chain by which I will no longer say that anything is impossible! I really do believe that we live in a world of incremental gain where we can change anything, or at least begin to change it.

A few years later I was out in Denver, and I heard some equally stupid people say: "You lucky people in St. Louis. But they'll never get it across the mountains." And then about three years ago we watched Telstar bouncing it off the satellite! The change in order of magnitude between Telstar and Denver was much greater than the magnitude between the football field and the parking lot and there to Denver. In the sense of an evolutionary bend, in the sense of an exponential curve, the real thing had happened even before I made a fool of myself. Some man had said. "You know, we've managed to get voice waves across the world. I wonder if we could do it with a picture." And everybody said: "You fool." And he said: "I wonder. I wonder. I wonder."

Today some students in some universities are beginning to say: "You know, we say all men are created equal. We say we're all children of God. We say all men are our brothers. We say that we believe in the mystical body of Christ. My parents have been telling me that, the papal encyclicals have been telling me that, the presidents of the United States have been telling me that. I wonder. I wonder. I wonder if it's possible."

And now I know that it will happen. My only ache is that I am not going to be around to see the fulfillment. A generation in their teens has begun to say "I wonder." Not just "I wonder if you can get a physical picture across the airways" but "I wonder, I wonder if the Red Chinese can ever search for reality with white Protestant Cincinnatians? I wonder, I wonder if one day the Viet Cong and a student from Webster College will be pursuing the same contemplative questions." And the minute we begin to say "I wonder" we have opened the floodgates to contemplation, we have opened the floodgates to pragmatism, we have opened the floodgates to becoming morally responsible to do a little bit. To do just a little bit. To do something, which is all we can do.

The third writer I want to share with you is not a Roman Catholic and not, therefore, a Jesuit. He's a professor of religion at Harvard. His name is Harvey Cox, and he has written a book with which I am fascinated called *The Secular City*. Harvey Cox is pleading for the world of secularization. Now if you're not careful, you'll think "She's already being heretical because all the Catholic newspapers warn us every day about secularism." Harvey Cox makes a very important distinction between secularism and secularization. He suggests that secularism is a closed ideology. And any closed ideology is always dangerous. Secularization, on the other hand, is a process of stripping the religious mythical notions from the other aspects of life. Cox maintains that man has proceeded from the tribe to the town to what he is now calling technopolis, the modern urban chain that goes down the length of California, the modern urban chain that is some day going to come from

Chicago to St. Louis. (The technological world must have a politics of its own.) But Cox says that as we have been going from the world of the tribe to the town to technopolis, we have also been going from the world of the myth to the world of ontology to the world of function, from the mythical age to the ontological age to the functional age. In the age of the tribe the tribesmen believed that everything had a one-to-one relationship to a god you named to dominate a specific thing. You didn't know how to explain it all so you created a sun god, a moon god, a cow god, and a grass god, because there was no way that evolutionary man had yet been permitted by his powers to find another kind of rationale. And so he got a one-to-one correspondence, and we had a really mythical world in the age of the tribe. In the age of the town, which corresponded in the Western world with the medieval synthesis, we inherited the tandem that Cox calls the junction tandem of Plato, Aristotle and Thomas which captured the gospel for a long time. We delivered the gospel to the world of ontology. The world of ontology was interested in essences, trying to define what goodness was, what truth was, what omniscience was, what omnipotence was, what infallibility was. Cox suggests that the Yawehist thinker of the Bible would never care about—he wouldn't even recognize—an ontological idea. He would say God is because of what God does. He brought me out of the land of bondage and into the land of Egypt. I know God by what he did for me, by what he did for man.

But now in the age of technopolis we are pragmatic men. We are living in a functional age and we say: What will men *do?* Some of us do not have very much patience with people who talk about human rights and then say it is the will of God for one race to be inferior to another, or that it is the will of God for somebody to be poor, really poor, and somebody

else to be rich. Some of us are beginning to wonder if maybe
that is wrong. And once somebody has begun to wonder, the
world is in turmoil. And so the world is in turmoil today.

Cox suggests that many of the religions are talking today
about ecumenicity. But many of them are talking about it in
awfully partial measures. He says it is now enormously popular in religious circles to talk about dialogue with the world.
Almost every conference of church workers must now include
some exposure to art, theaters, or politics, usually carefully in-
troduced and interpreted. The sentiment is commendable, but
the reality is a caricature of dialogue with the world. What
happens is that the churches try to understand and confront
the world on the churches' terms and in the churches' language. Churches have an uncanny capacity to emasculate criticism simply by modifying it and then incorporating it into
the continuous but ineffectual self-flagellation that goes on in
all organizations. Last year's most critical blast turns up as the
study theme for next year's women's circles! Attacks on the
caution of the churches can often reach a fever pitch in discussions among denominational executives, after which the
executives return to more or less the same pursuits. These safe
little family sessions of criticism serve the same purpose as
hurling an ashtray across the room—they let off steam without
really changing anything. They may allow church functions to
remain sane, but they do less than nothing to alter the structure in which they are entrapped because they give the de-
ceptive appearance that something is really happening.

Then Cox goes on to discuss the church in the modern university, the concern which is most meaningful to my own soul.
Cox says the anachronistic posture of churches of all kinds is
nowhere more obvious than in the context of the university
community. The establishment of its own colleges and universities by a church, Cox says, is of course medievalism. The

whole idea of a Christian college or university after the breaking apart of the medieval synthesis has little meaning. The
term *Christian* is not one that can be used to refer to universities any more than to observatories or laboratories. No one
of the so-called Christian colleges that now dot our Midwest
is able to give a very plausible theological basis for retaining
the phrase *Christian college* in the catalogue. Granted that
there may be excellent traditional public relations or sentimental reasons for calling a college Christian, but there are no
theological reasons. A college may have been founded by
ministers, or have a certain number of Christians on the faculty or in the student body. Chapel may or may not be required, or the college may have part of its bill paid by a de-
nomination. None of these factors provides any grounds for
labeling an institution with a word that the Bible applies only
to the followers of Christ, to persons, and then very spar-
ingly. Cox suggests that the idea of developing Christian universities in America was bankrupt even before it began. I
recount his position to you not because I completely believe
it. I am still running a Catholic college. But I read it to you
because it hits me where my own vested interest is the deepest.

I spoke at Brandeis a couple of years ago, and a group of
young theologians, Jesuits from Weston, came to talk to me.
They began to write to me shortly after that and later published an article in *America*. These young Jesuits who had not
yet been ordained were beginning to worry about the investment of the Jesuits in brick and mortar. They said: "Do you
know, Sister, that we Jesuits teach fifty per cent of the college
students who are now in the Catholic colleges and universities? So we ought to be the men who are most ready to go
play the secular university apostolate." They are probably
more ready as a group to go fight for positions at Harvard,
Yale, and Radcliffe, Dartmouth, Minnesota, and Ohio than

anybody else in the world. They have good enough credentials to go get them. "But," said these young men, "we are chained by our institutions. We own them all and nobody knows what to do with them."

And so today I am struggling with all my might and main to get the Sisters of Loretto to yield the ownership of Webster College. I do not believe—I, personally, with a finite human mind which may be wrong—I personally do not believe that colleges and universities ought to be owned and operated by religious orders. I believe that colleges and universities ought to be staffed partially by persons who belong to religious orders. We ought to be everywhere where action is. Cox says that modern Christianity ought to be like a floating crap game—you go where the action is. And if any of you have seen a not-so-good musical comedy called *Guys and Dolls* you know there is one wonderful interlude in it where the floating crap game goes into the sewers.

But unless we are free, unless we travel light, unless we believe the essential message of the gospel, which is "detachment," we are going to be owned by our institutions. And I personally say that I won't spend my life defending the institutional framework, because I think it has destroyed Christianity. We are in the minority, and that is all right. There ought to be people here who disbelieve us very strongly. We will either win humanity by the power structure, which often turns into the power *stricture*, or we will win humanity by the input of our power, by the input of grace.

Why did John XXIII have such a transcendent, transforming effect upon the world? Because he loved it. Because he opened himself to all men, because he got inside the skin of all men, because almost every man in the world, if he had the chance, would have run into his arms, because John somehow or other was not afraid. If we can revive this again in the

Christian message, we can believe what grace is—that grace dwells inside ourselves and that it is the life of God, the power of God. The reformation and the counter-reformation are over, the day of apologia is over, the day of the debating societies is over, but the day of contemplation and wonder is here again. That means, I think, that I must share in inquiry with a Hindu, an atheist, and a Protestant. And—just as important—*they* must share with *me*.

The ecumenical world of search is an alternating current, a two-way, many-way street. When I learned about ecumenism as a little girl in Sterling, Illinois, I learned about an ecumenism that I held in my hand. I patted somebody on the head and I said to him: "Now, look, we've got it all. If I just pray for you long enough, you'll open up your hardened heart, and I'll hand it to you." How awful, how smug, how arrogant, how stupid. We must be able to tell people that we're bothered, that we're troubled, that we're contemplative, that we are finite men struggling with the infinite—an infinite we will never reach, because to be finite men struggling with the infinite is to struggle toward a moving limit. If we say that to them, they will again open up their own hearts.

Cox says there is no such thing as a general atheist. An atheist is only an atheist against a particular concept of God. If we produce a concept of God that is mechanistic, our moral code of mechanistic materialism will make many atheistic Communist systems look pale by comparison. If a parish community or a college community or a religious community offers a syndrome of judgment that's left over from Puritan culture which indulged in witchcraft trials, that community ought to die. Because the Christian life is the empathic life; is the compassionate life; is the open life. Read the gospel.

The only persons Christ was ever hard on were the Pharisees, who were the mechanistic materialists of their religious day. They were hypocrites; they were hard on everybody else. What did he say to the woman taken in adultery? He said to that group of Pharisees: "Let him who is without guilt cast the first stone." And he wrote something in the sand and never told us what it was. And he said: "Is no man going to condemn her?" And they said: "No man, Lord." And remember the next line: "They walked away, beginning with the eldest." Christ was always compassionate. The Pharisees found fault with the Christ for dealing with Mary Magdalen; they found fault with the Christ for dealing with the tax-gatherer, just as now the Catholic laity find fault with nuns who go out at night. Each group is building an expectancy behavior code for every other group.

My father, who never finished high school and is a farmer in Illinois, a beautiful human being, was talking to a group of nuns about this business of judgment. He said: "You can afford to judge only the people you love. But unfortunately we usually do it the other way. We make our judgments against the people we don't love and we don't know." Then he told a lovely story: "You know, there were some Irish fellows working on a sewer in front of a house of ill repute. They looked down the street, and there was a young rabbi. And the young rabbi came down the street and walked into that house. And Pat said: 'Glory be to God, the man of God has come to this!' And they were still working on the sewer a few days later when the young Episcopal clergyman walked down the street and he turned in that same door. And Pat looked at Mike and said: 'The whole world has gone to pot—it has come to the whole of the religious!' It must have been a bad sewer, because they were still working on it a few days later. And the young curate from St. Michael's walked down the street and in the door. And Pat looked at Mike, and he said: 'Glory be to God, Mike, I wonder which of the girls is ill?' "

It's an anecdote my father deserves to tell. My father seldom acts any other way. My father always believes that you don't know all the facts in the case, and that you always give people the benefit of the doubt. And so if I'm a Christian today, I'm a Christian in grace power because my father and mother breathed it into me. Because they continue to breathe it into me. They protected me from much of the legalism of mechanistic materialism and made me ready to go out into an ecumenical world of search.

The world is full of conservatives who want liberal results. The world is full of people who want the revenue of the blue-chip stocks with four and a half per cent savings' security. You may many times have to invest in the four and a half per cent savings' security, but please admit it. If you want to invest your child in the great Christian drama, in the great human drama, you must let him take chances. You cannot indoctrinate him, you cannot give him his foundations and build up a fortress and then tell him to go respond to that world.

I believe that God gave us free will. I believe that He is the great and loving one who stands at the top of the hill with His hands out. That is the kind of college administrator I would like to be. That is the kind of mother of a family I would like to be if I could live that life the next time around. That is the kind of President of the United States I would like to be if I were good enough to make it. That is the kind of Bishop I would like to be if I could make it, because only compassion can make responsible human beings. We cannot do it halfway. The world can no longer live divided. The world will evolve into a beautiful new world in somebody's generation if we have real trust that all men can search together. That, I think, is the ecumenical world of search. And if there is a heaven, and I believe there is—though I haven't a ghost of a show of what it's going to be like—we will all meet there.

And I will love you, and you will love me, even if you would like to hang me tonight.

Can the academic world seek the living God?

Vassar College
Poughkeepsie, New York
December 4, 1967

The selectivity process of memory is interesting indeed. The imagination keeps retrieving from the memory bits of conversation, lines from plays, snatches of music. Often it is a one-time shot called up by a specific experience at the moment. Sometimes, though, one such piece of conversation or one such dramatic line keeps recurring at the oddest times. Like all analogies or poetic metaphors, the line and the experience have just that degree of overlapping identity or mirror symmetry that makes their combination more interesting than either one alone.

In recent years, the memory of Molière's *bourgeois gentilhomme* has recurrently intruded on my imagination with his wonderfully naïve discovery that prose was what he had been speaking all the time.

The world of scholarship and the world of poetic discovery

are, I am sure, children of the same intellectual mother, but they are often brother and sister temporarily out of synchronization with one another. We have long known that the joy of surprise and the joy of recognition are separate and distinct and reinforcing joys. In a flash of insight one puts together the heretofore unmembered pieces of a mathematical theorem, of a poem becoming, of a political decision. Out of the travail of the day-to-day and year-to-year non-sense of one's life, one begins to evolve a way of viewing, a mode of acting, a philosophy of living. Personally, individually, uniquely, it is *your* way of viewing, *your* mode of acting, *your* philosophy of living—just as it was *your* mathematical theorem, *your* poem becoming, *your* political decision.

Then one day, the masters of erudition and scholarship begin to annotate your papers or corner you at cocktail parties demanding to know if your position is not derived from that of Socrates, or that of Tillich, or that of Bergson. Unless one gauges that the erudite and scholarly questioner has a sense of humor, a sense of the dignity but also of the partialness of scholarship, one had better not admit one's often partial and sometimes total lack of familiarity with the suggested scholarly ancestor of one's current thought.

Recently, both letter-writing and cocktail-party inquisitors —with and without a scholarly sense of humor—have been badgering me to declare my dependence on Bergson. I finally acknowledged to a bright young philosopher on my faculty that it was about time I broke down and found out if it were Bergson I had been speaking all the time. And so I am reading Bergson with my quite junior faculty member. (His version is quite probably that he is tutoring me.)

Already, it is obvious to me that I would recognize Bergson if I met him in written or spoken conversation. At the risk of real and/or perceived arrogance, I believe he would also have recognized me, had the scholarly interpreters of each and both not filled the air with the overpowering noise of their interpretations.

In recent years, I have been preoccupied with the question of morality, of the personal responsibility for one's actions. When, then, Bergson talks about the morality of pressure representing a society which aims only at self-preservation and distinguishes this from a morality of aspiration which implicitly contains the feeling of progress, I know that we have shared a fundament of experience which makes for recognition. The recognition is full of both hope and frustration as I hear him saying: "Precisely because we find ourselves in the presence of the ashes of an extinct emotion, and because the driving power of that emotion came from the fear within it, the formulae which have remained would generally be incapable of rousing our will," unless in stirring the ashes, "we shall find some of them stiill warm, and at length the sparks will kindle into flame." In this context he sees founders and reformers of religion, mystics and saints as souls opening out, breaking with nature; he sees heroism as possibly the only way to love, heroism as a return to movement, emanating from an emotion—"infectious like all emotions—akin to a creative art."

I am already involved in a basic contradiction. I led into this discussion with an obvious value judgment—thinly veiled as a distinction—a value judgment in favor of the world of poetic discovery over the world of scholarship. Having shot my barbs at the humorless sector of erudition, I have in real sophomoric style trotted out my beginning research findings in reading a very profound man. Should I apologize? If life and truth are linear and logical, indeed I should. If, instead, life and truth are nonlinear, dynamic, multidimensional, paradoxical, and metaphorical, then instead I posit my seeming contradictions, my unfinished puzzle as a true moment if not as a moment of truth.

Human learning, viable insight is, I believe, always the word made flesh in *a* person, incorporated, incarnated in a person. Data are present in random form in natural and man-made phenomena. Data are available in books and computers in selective edited form. Insight into the data and into the meaning of the pattern or patterns suggested by the data is incorporated by a person and becomes at best and at worst a hypothesis to be incorporated in whole or in part by other human persons.

Let us look briefly at the world of science—the world of modern man—as a world of invention. Is it a world of simple obsolescence? Is it a world that is true today only if it discovers and discloses the error of yesterday?

If we look at the world of technology—the transportation, communications, mechanical and electrical power systems (or especially the technological artifacts that make up those systems at any given time), then it is certainly a world of obsolescence. The inventions of today are discarded in the ashcans, the junk heaps of tomorrow. The new civilization of today, aided by the bulldozer or the artifact that makes the bulldozer obsolete, will become an archeological layer buried by the next stratum of technological development.

Do civilizations, then, destroy one another so that new inventors may replace them with new forms? Is history best represented in the disjunction of synthetic artifacts or in the continuity, reproduction, and transformation of organic life? What is the tension between discontinuity and continuity in the life of an individual person, in the life of a college or university, in the life of a nation, in the life of a church? The minute I choose "life" as the character not only of the person but also of his institutions, I have already characterized his institutions as possessing at least potential continuity by reproducing and transforming themselves in a quasi-organic life.

But—if human learning, viable insight, is always the word made flesh in *a* person, is always incorporated in *a* person, how can colleges or nations or churches learn? How can institutions read the data accumulated in their histories and present in their institutional worlds and in the worlds beyond their institutions? Even more difficult, how can institutions see into and beyond these data and discover the patterns presented by the data so that the new conceptions of reality are at once richer and more freighted with ambiguity even as they attempt to simplify and clarify that reality?

And still more difficult, how do institutions incarnate these developing conceptions into the body of man, the people of God? How is the word made flesh in the body politic?

Joan Baez and Joey Bishop debate respect and responsibility, peace and murder in the midnight of television in Southern California. Robert McNamara becomes expendable to the Johnson administration—or does the administration become expendable to Robert McNamara? Robert Kennedy assaults the simple-minded anticommunism which is the moral rectitude of the students at his wife's alma mater. This is the same—or is he the same—Robert Kennedy who once seemed to embody some of the words of Senator Joseph McCarthy. And a different Senator McCarthy in what he sees as loyalty to his party announces his candidacy in opposition to the incumbent party leader.

Newspaper headlines disclose that the Viet Cong made aborative efforts to bring their case to the UN General Assembly and that the United States would "entertain" them only—interestingly enough—in the Security Council. And the White House calls it a false report. And we wonder first if the particular report is accurate or inaccurate; and, more important, if the contextual pattern of emerging data makes such a report likely or unlikely in fact or in possibility?

Augustine pondered over the city of God. Today we ponder over the city of the universe—the tangled, noisy, fragmented, diseased, warring world of alienated or unrecognized brothers for whom the "family of man" is obviously a word not yet made flesh, a theological conception perhaps true and safe as a theoretical abstraction, but subject not only to crucifixion but to infanticide if it somehow begins to become incarnate in the city of the universe.

And all the time—as persons here and there attempt to conceive and make fecund the family of man, to nurture the embryo lest it recurringly abort itself in an alien environment—you and your peers live in another smaller university world which to a large degree still operates as its own security council in power-preservation over and against the general assembly of the madding crowd. In the name of scholarship, in the name of rigor, in the name of intellectual discipline the university continues to demand its own research designs, carefully keeping out of the laboratory—the controlled environment of the contrived university—the tangled, fragmented, diseased elements of the city of the universe. We introduce the theoretical abstractions and conceptions, the *words* in the university world—but the word made flesh—the flesh that will make for the new insights, the new conceptions is not always or even often appropriate to our rigorous research designs.

If we train teachers through theoretical abstractions to "play the game" in the military mode of most inner-city systems, we will contribute to the pile of ashes of an extinct emotion. On the other hand, if we involve teachers in inventing curriculum and devising new processes of working with children in the sanctuary-utopia of our contrived university, we should not be surprised if our small sparks are soon smothered by the ashes of the system.

Only the fire kindled and fanned in the soggy wood of the market place can warm that market place. Only the continuing involvement of faculty and students within a university in the tangled, fragmented, diseased elements of the city of the universe can keep the flame of relevance informing the theoretical abstractions.

I do not believe it is enough that faculty stay "current" by reading the latest articles in the journal and inserting current and relevant comments in their lectures or Socratic discussions. The professor and his student must find ways as action-intellectuals of continuing to systematize from relevant experience conceptual formulations, insightful perceptions of pattern.

If the student is to be liberalized, freed to be such an action-intellectual, he must be allowed and pressed to share in the search for new patterns in the market place, even as he commits to the data bank of his own memory the formulations of other men of other times. Only so, I believe, can he respect the achievement and the fallibility of other formulations as he recognizes in his own attempts the necessary partialness and incompleteness of the inductive process which produced the formula.

There is on the wall of my office a beautiful black-and-white photograph made to show how waves can be brought to a focus by a lens. I had long admired it on the wall of a very dear friend who is a physicist. He sent it to me with a long footnote which means much to me because it captures, for me at least, a view of the world, a way of knowing, a philosophy of living that he—out of his formation as an empirical scientist who is an agnostic—and I—out of my world of formation in religious commitment—have come to share at a profound level.

Let me share at least the words with you, in the hope that they can summon up for you an image of the photograph:

> This picture was made to show how waves can be brought to a focus by a lens. The waves are produced (near the bottom of the photograph) in a shallow layer of water as plane or straight lines—as though they were produced by a source of waves far, far away. In the ideal case of a large lens (large means simply many times larger than the distance between the waves) the focus would appear sharp and the waves, after passing the focus, would spread radially to form circular waves of ever expanding radius. But, as always, we have no ideal conditions. The focus is not sharp —the waves, after focus, are not circular, and the pattern is not clear. But a sort of focus is visible and a spreading of the distorted waves is apparent.
>
> But what is the moral of this story? If the wavelength were shorter, if the subject of an issue is narrow, then even with an eye of small scope we can obtain some clarity. And for large issues, of great wavelength, we need vision or lenses of large scope, if we want our focus or image clear.
>
> But we must learn from small issues something about the nature of sharp focus. Then maybe we can broaden our lenses and broaden our issues.
>
> This is a lesson from science.

I would rather say this is a lesson from a scientist-humanist, *his* insight into a meaning suggested by the picture and by other phenomena—many of which I have shared, an insight shared with me in the process and the fact of its incarnation, shared now with you in the hope that you may incorporate it in some form into the whole of my sharing with you and into the way of viewing, the mode of acting, the philosophy of living that is peculiarly yours.

The insight, precisely because of its tension truth, its grasp of paradox, is helpful in our attempt to understand the dilemma and the potential power of the modern world of higher education. Unless we respect the discipline and the rigor represented by the world of research design, by the world of scholarship, by the world of deductive reasoning, we will never bring to our poetic insights the sharp focus and we will never learn the process of sharp focus by which, one day, we will invent the larger and more powerful lenses with which we can broaden our issues.

Yet the issues do not wait for the invention of the lenses. Indeed, perhaps only the perception of a sort of focus and the spreading of the distorted waves can provoke us to attempt to make the new lenses.

Poetic paradox is seeming contradiction—and yet, when it is successful, we sense its profound trueness. In the art form of poetry it comes to us in the integrity of the artifact that is the poem. In the city of the universe, and probably in the university, it comes to us only through the distorted waves. When a sort of focus is visible, we are sometimes tantalized and sometimes terrified by what a broadened lens might see. We are, at the same time, if we are bright, somewhat put off by the dogged determination that must go into the invention of the new lens.

I think I share to some degree with many contemporary students their impatience with contrived and irrelevant deductive systems. At the same time, I see and want to see myself as an idealistic pragmatist, as a humanistic political actionist. Within this commitment, I am daily more convinced that rigor and discipline must be held in continuing tension with heuristic vision and poetic insight. If they are held in such continuing tension in the life of an individual or in the life of an institution, they will periodically lose their tension integration in given actions. Unless, however, the person or the community of persons that make up the institution have both the faith and the agnosticism to live with the tension, they will study photographs of static pictures, but they will not train their lenses on that which lies beyond.

I have no clear focus of the life-style of the community of persons who comprise an institution. The spreading of the distorted waves says only to me that theirs is a *life*-style only if we see an institution as such a community of persons, not as an artifact in itself. The insights, both deductive and inductive, of these persons are shared with other persons—not only as completed poems, but also in the process of looking at the distorted waves. In this process, search for words becomes flesh (and even two-in-one flesh) as the community of persons struggle for new conceptions.

This, to me, is the mystery of the incarnation, the word made flesh, the divine life, the divine spark, continually being incarnated in the person of man and in the family of man who must build up the city of the universe. Only to the degree that there is such a city will there be a city of God. Only the secular city can incorporate the divine life, the divine spark.

Formal theology will return to the secular university and the living God will return to the city of the universe only if we can begin to live with the paradox of agnosticism and faith, only if we can begin to live with the wonder and terror of knowing and not knowing, because a living man, a living community, like any concept or reality of a living God, is beyond the grasp of framed photographs, beyond the grasp of finished formulation, beyond the grasp of dogmatic closure.

But precisely so are they not within the grasp and search of persons and communities of persons who allow themselves to live in the tension integration, and disintegration of agnosticism and faith?

If modern man can reincarnate within his pragmatic self, if university professors can reincarnate within their rigorous (and sometimes cynical) selves a sense of wonder and of contemplation, then indeed we may be able to broaden our issues in the city of the universe and in the university. The secular view which has stripped us of one kind of magic-myth may open us to the really wondrous pursuit of the unknown which is beyond our grasp, beyond our measurements, beyond our individual academic disciplines, beyond our particular institutions.

The quest for ultimates—which is called by some the quest for the living God—must, I believe, become again the fascinating and baffling quest of the family of man if there is within the members of the family the power of the sons of God.

About Jacqueline Grennan

Jacqueline Grennan is a graduate of Webster College in Missouri, which she now heads as president. Miss Grennan became a member of the Order of the Sisters of Loretto in 1950. As Sister Jacqueline she taught in secondary schools, receiving her master's degree at the University of Notre Dame in 1957. In 1959 she began her career at Webster College as assistant to the president, and later became vice president in charge of development. National publicity came as a result of the experimental education program she devised. In 1967 Miss Grennan simultaneously announced her decision to transfer the control of Webster—a Catholic women's college—to a lay board, and to request dispensation from her vows in the Order. Both moves were approved by the Church. Honored by and participating in many organizations, Miss Grennan has been a member of the President's Advisory Panel on Education since 1963, and also serves as a consultant to Head Start and the Peace Corps.